MY SUNSHINE
for Rainy Days

MY SUNSHINE
for Rainy Days

Kevin Alan Lamb

Copyright © 2026 Kevin Alan Lamb.

All rights reserved. No part of this publication may be reproduced, distributed, or transmitted in any form or by any means, including photocopying, recording, or other electronic or mechanical methods, without the prior written permission of the publisher, except in the case of brief quotations embodied in critical reviews and certain other noncommercial uses permitted by copyright law. For permission requests, write to the publisher, addressed "Attention: Permissions Coordinator," at the address below.

Printed by KDP, in the United States of America. First printing edition 2026.

Caffeine, Dreams, & Love Publishing
490 Lakes Edge Drive
Oxford, MI. 48371

ISBN: 979-8-9947320-0-7 (Paperback)

Also by Kevin Alan Lamb

Ele Phan-Te
Love Vigilante
Love Is in the Details
Your Daily Guide to Shine
The Dying Romantic

For those who choose to look inward for courage, instead of looking away from injustice. For those who use their voice to speak on others' behalf. For a better America than we know today.

If you're waiting for the right time, there won't be one. If you're waiting on someone, you'll always be. If you need help, ask for it. If you don't believe in it, find something that you do. Once you've bled for something, it changes you. Hunger is a powerful force. Dreams don't need to be forced—but if you hear it calling—stay the course. Impossible is a limited perspective. Lost causes are waiting to be found. Pages beg to be written. You're given dreams for a reason. Somewhere they've already come true. The divine expresses itself through you. God sees through your eyes. Love grows with the beat of your heart. You are the hero of this story. Only you can decide what is worth saving. Only you can decide to keep going. Only you can find what you're looking for. And only you know what it's supposed to feel like when you've found it.

– My Sunshine, for Rainy Days

Valentine's Day in Bad Axe
back in Michigan's thumb to retreat and relax
better learning to enjoy each of the seasons
dancing with them until they pass
another winter weather advisory in the forecast
safely nestled in our cabin in the woods
spikes of ice formed from falling water
frozen in place, slowly growing with the days
thankful for another Star Forest Stay
have you ever taken a winter retreat?
letting yourself grow in love with the people you meet
lending faith to the unknown helps you believe
we get what we deserve, in time you'll see
loving yourself, sets you free
only your heart knows who you're meant to be
let us embrace snow storms and dwell in the trees
stoic in nature, virtuous, and at peace
observing the miracle of breath helps us breathe
snowed in, Port Austin, with everything we need
taking time, setting intentions,
infusing life by planting seeds

(winter retreat)

Winter comes for each of us in its own way. As I drink my morning coffee, I look out my window in awe of its luminescence, blanketing the land. Under my blanket—in my brown reclining chair—I have about 30 minutes before it starts to hurt my lower back (it's kind of a shitty chair). For two-and-a-half years I've started my days this way: looking out at the water (ice), listening to music softly, seeing where my keystrokes take me. Morning has become my favorite time of day to write while observing nature's stillness through my window to the world. It's a little surreal that next week I will be publishing my third book in three years, but then again, this is the writer's perch I always dreamed of. I've never owned a home—nor do I particularly care to—but my, how I often longed for this very view from which I now gaze each morning, afternoon, and night. The conditions of our environment can play a major role in our productivity, creativity, flow, and success. I think everyone should give themselves the opportunity to experience what they perceive as their ideal conditions. There's often more ways to realize your goals than the obvious or traditional path. For example, I was no longer satisfied with my inability to answer the question "Kevin, why don't you live on water?" Michigan is surrounded by the Great Lakes, and second only to Minnesota with roughly eleven thousand inland lakes. Later that day I found a room for rent with a lake view on Craigslist. It was the first and only place I looked at. Come June, it will have been three years. All of this is to say, maybe the ideal conditions for whatever it is you hope to create are closer, and more attainable than you think. Maybe, you just need to look at it from a slightly different

continued

continued

angle. Winter is that way: it can be cold, heavy, dark, and inconvenient, but maybe it's time you try to consider it from a different perspective. Maybe, it's giving you the time and space you asked for to heal. Maybe, it's one more nudge in the direction of creating something you've too long let go to your wayside. Maybe, it's picking up the phone to have a conversation that's the first step in repairing a relationship with someone you love. It's easy and relatively common to blame the weather, the government, or other people for our problems, but it rarely helps. Most of the answers we seek, and love we long for resides inside you and I. With 28 days remaining until spring—rather than simply enduring winter—try to take a look at your life from a slightly different perspective, and either make some changes or remember how much of your daily life is a blessing you once asked for. Either way, each of us has a responsibility to play an active role in our disposition and lens through which we see the world.

(28 days until spring)

And just like that, another decade well lived. To say it's gone by would undermine and overlook just how marvelous these last ten years have been. I wear each of my forty years as a badge of honor, gratitude, and majestic colors that paint my aura wild and spectacular. Somewhere along the way it became crystal clear to me that joy and enthusiasm are perceived as youth, and most people are drawn to their magnetism. When operating from a place of curiosity and excitement, we have the tendency to see solutions where others identify problems. We take the time and intention to notice the subtle and miraculous nature within the patterns that weave our experiences, relationships, and environment together into a fluid stream. By letting go of the man I once was—along with visions of the man I ought to be—I continue to let myself grow into the man that I am. Without reservation or hesitation I am proud of the man I've become. I've said it before and I'll say it again: I've walked my five hundred miles, lived my 10k hours, and emerged on the other side with a smile and resilience in tow. In 1967 Dr. Martin Luther King Jr. wrote his final book, "Where Do We Go From Here: Chaos or Community?" Not even two months into 2025, each of us has been given a better understanding of chaos, and it is my hope that with it—we've been reminded how dearly

continued

continued

we need community. Somehow, someway, it's been 58 years since Dr. King wrote his last book—isolated in a house in Jamaica—yet our struggle for freedom and equality in the United States endures. Where has our curiosity, generosity, and excitement gone as a people? Which god of yours sold you on the notion of scarcity, judgement, and possession? What promises could be so appealing that we abandon reason, decency, and love? Have you ever thought to consider our potential if we didn't waste so much time and energy fighting amongst ourselves? What might be possible if we programmed ourselves to see solutions in the place of problems? Common bonds in the place of our differences? Your disdain and distaste for others is not pleasant dinner conversation, nor a positive example for your children, or grandchildren. We as a people face great adversity, why not embrace it as a community? Naturally, there will always be those who choose chaos—and we must choose to love them anyway or let them go. In the face of chaos I walk in the other direction and find those who choose community. I choose those who seek a path of qualitative growth and expansion, trusting that together we will build, provide, and offer others—shelter from the storm. May your voice be heard, but

continued

continued

have something to say. May you know the comfort of love, by first loving others. May your dreams become realities, so long as they benefit others. May your prayers be answered, so long as they help others. May you hold youth in your heart, by first letting your love guide you in the direction of curiosity and excitement. May we as a people: human beings with hopes, dreams, and fears—choose community over chaos and hate. I may or may not have another forty years, but in what time that does remain—I hope we can remember where we came from, and what our lives might look like without the love, generosity, and sacrifice others made on our behalf.

(chaos or community?)

The birds return to the trees before the leaves, where they sing their morning songs and revel in the final breaths of winter. Yesterday delivered our first glimpse of the coming spring, blanketed in sunshine and 50 degrees—alas the lake begins to unfreeze. We say our goodbyes to February, thankful for its epic snowfall and restoration of the earth below. We welcome March: new beginnings, new life, and growth. Twenty-three days until spring, and still every day—the birds sing. Nature's music is ripe with lessons begging us to listen. Slow down and be thankful, while blessings are being readied by your angels. Ask, and you shall receive. Having faith requires that you believe; in something bigger than yourself. You don't have to do it by yourself. Don't be so worried about all of those times you slipped and fell. Somehow you always seem to forget that each of those times you slipped, you found your back to your feet. Each time with a little less help. You've grown stronger with the days—facing fears in your own way—learning you don't have to be so afraid. Others will be there for you the way you have been there for them. Helping hands await your wants and needs. It's alright to ask for help. It's imperative that we ask for help. Most of us need to learn how to better ask for help. Try not to expect other people to help. Remember to be grateful, when people help. Pay it forward if you can. Pay it

continued

continued

forward when you can. Be thankful for helping hands. Remind yourself they enjoy being of use. Hard work is therapy in the form of truth. Evidence in becoming. The joy of running. Believing in something. Acting upon belief. Understanding wants from needs. Cutting your teeth. Building a foundation. Working from the ground up. Accompanied by the sound of birds returning to the trees before the leaves. Singing their morning songs. Reveling in the final breaths of winter. Thankful yesterday delivered our first glimpse of the coming spring. Don't be so worried about all of those times you slipped and fell, here you are on your feet again.

(from the ground up)

I woke this morning to the rise of a blood moon shining through the window on my face. It felt as though a familiar friend was greeting me to say everything is going to be okay. With my window slightly open to start my day, sounds and signs of spring pour through in the form of honking geese, a warm breeze, and birds fluttering in the trees. Today's high is 67 degrees, yet the lake remains still, briefly holding its freeze. Light, wispy clouds cascade upon the sky of blue, listen as your higher self speaks to you. For some it may be a whisper, for others a picturesque dream—a Total Lunar Eclipse urging us to release what no longer serves us—embrace new beginnings, and have faith in the unseen. May we let go of the pain we carry, let in the love we seek, and embrace this cosmic reset—open to receive soul's next steps. It's been a long, hard winter, I understand it's difficult to imagine giving your best. I hope you can give yourself some time this weekend, to pause and rest. I have great admiration for all those who find a way to carry on amidst hard times, without abandoning the warmth and kindness that helps them shine. We need that kindness more than ever. Cretins and fools have gone to war with empathy, but rather than give them our anger, hate, or sympathy, I hope we can come together in kindness—once more discovering unity. Through oppression, tyranny, and

continued

continued

degradation by a heavy ruling hand without empathy—each of us has a better understanding of what's at stake—and who is really in our corner when it comes to goodness sake. It turns out it's people like you and I, doing their best to stay afloat, terrified how the land of the free so quickly gave way to our current reality. But in our shared struggle we once more become brother, sister, neighbor, ally, and friend. As we lay low, heal, lick our wounds, rest and regroup, the universe has taken the lead— aligned the planets and given us a blood moon. Take your breaths, give yourself what you really *need*, and look for the courage that will help you hold onto faith—because it doesn't take much to know that this isn't the way. Plain as day we see who isn't serving us, maybe that's the nudge we need to put our trust in love. If you're breathing and above ground, that's enough momentum for a better way to be found. You don't need to have the answers—to alleviate cancers—and please don't abandon your hope nor dreams, after all, faith is grounded in the unseen.

(blood moon)

Seasons change before the weather does
growth welcomes something better for us
everyday choices giving our intentions voices
building on a foundation that continues to last
raising the vibration to meet what we've asked
letting go of what and who has come to pass
trusting the four winds to blow us in the right direction
some miracles are merely a matter of perspective
are you willing to hold space for the unexpected?
try to remember all the times your faith has been tested
consider the source of the strength you've invested
the alchemy from which darkness became light
holding on for life, until love was in sight
holding on until others, did what is right
seasons change before the weather does
growth welcomes something better for us
kindness cures what's aching in us
love protects what hate tries to take from us
spring's rebirth and renewal require trust
mother nature blesses us with pollen and pixie dust
teaching us to slow down, be patient, and lead with love

(mother alchemy)

Maybe it's just about your time to shine
maybe you've been preparing yourself for something better
maybe you decided you're tired of holding yourself back
maybe you're ready for something bigger
maybe you're ready for someone sweeter
maybe you just need to worry a little less
maybe people noticed you always doing your best
maybe you learned to let go and rest
maybe patience was the test
maybe love comes next
maybe hard work pays off
maybe resilience blooms
maybe flowers grow
maybe it all works out
maybe it all comes together
maybe you just needed to learn to shine
no matter the weather

(maybe love comes next)

Even gray days are colorful when it's warm
urging us to welcome in something more
aiming our sights higher than we have before
trusting our time would eventually come
thankful wolves taught us how to run
mindful we've outlasted some
hopeful for the journey ahead
grateful for the journey behind
holding close this heart of mine
knowing there comes a time to shine
even if most days feel like we're standing still
building endurance, ascending hills
shedding relationships, trauma, and weight
letting go to make some space
endurance is the name of the game
learning how dreams are made
a recipe of necessity
a taste of what it takes
to build and be something great
open and hoping to receive
answered prayers and the love we need

(recipe of necessity)

March, you were different this year
probably because I'm different this year
downshifting gears, letting go of the wheel
operating from flow and feel
bearing witness to the songs and sounds
the music of my soul reveals
playing in my own way
standing on my own stage
daydreaming, wide awake
helping others for goodness sake
giving more than I take
mindful of the wake my words create
visible ripples made dimples in smiles
tangible tears shed from eyes in grief
love in the form of a moment's relief
life in the belief that it's worth holding on to
peace in the hearts of the stars and stripes
empathy in the hands of he rolling the dice
staying the course amid long, dark nights
showing up for humanity, or learning the price
helping hands, kindness, and being nice
mean more to one another right now
than you think they might

(march)

The choice to begin April
with a hopeful and gracious heart
waking up with hot tea and Emerson
an awe-inspiring American scholar with resonance
clarity and guidance without pretension
doing the right thing without mention
breaking free of institution and convention
unburdened by the ego of men unburdened with ascension
water makes no distinction of who it rises with its tide
love knows no borders untouched by the divine
spirit lifts all those who acknowledge it inside
hands help all those who to a heart guides
may a man be measured by who he unites
rather than those who he divides
let us practice decency over hateful pride
there will never be a better time
to choose humanity and shine
light and life into cold, dark places
offering warmth and smiles to the faces
of those who deserve to know
that being helped is essential to grow
and we musn't forget
that we only get what we give

(get what we give)

The 2nd of April feels like 9 degrees
black birds chirp, feeding in leafless trees
a single swan patrols the lake
spring winds blow cascading waves
sleet with intermittent rain
not likely to see the sun today
so we shine from the inside out
writing poetry in protest of the heartless
practicing stillness to combat illness
observing birds to find the words
to paint pictures of divinity
spirit moves through nature
giving it that ability
walking a fine line between
stability and fragility
powerful and powerless
their songs suggest bliss
at flight and at play
singing in the rain
grateful for today

(singing in the rain)

Each of us must
do our best not to be discouraged
learning why they call it courage
learning we have a choice
learning to listen to our own voice
observing without absorbing the noise
grace and elegance bear poise
faith and trust transcend time
consider your departure from the grind
look inward for guidance from the divine
a cosmic treasure map buried inside
a letter to yourself from the other side
intuition is instruction and guide
gravitational pull to turn the tide
answering nature's call to rise
remembering we're grateful to be alive
each precious breath under blue skies
doing our best not to be discouraged
learning why they call it courage
learning we have a voice
will you sing harmony?
or be but another noise?

(call it courage)

Opening Day in Detroit
tigers ready to make some noise
jack flaherty on the hill
$100 tickets, still Comerica fills
gametime temperature of 49 degrees
navy blue and orange, fill the streets
father & sons, mothers & daughters
at the ballpark making new memories
the White Sox away from Comiskey
april sunshine and a cool breeze
home white and navy jerseys
first pitch from comedian
southfield's Keegan-Michael Key
it's a great day for baseball in the D
will it be consecutive playoff runs?
in time and September we'll see
but this Tigers fan believes
readily soaking in the poetry
of Jason Benetti and Dan Petry
hot starts from Riley Greene and Spenny T
in a first place tie with four teams
the boys of summer, america's pastime
the only diamond really worth a dime
blessed by Cecil, Sparky and Kaline
another season of faith's perfection
with only one way to have a happy ending

(opening day)

The scope of my work has blessed me with experiences and relationships that exceed many single lifetimes. I've never taken these blessings for granted, and in many instances they've been the staying power I've needed on a path that is anything but conventional—yet quite certainly my destiny. The quality of the love I've been given in places I had never been, by people who I had never met, and may never see again—has been the rocket fuel in my pursuit of the dreams in my heart. Many of these people, relationships, and experiences unknowingly leave their imprint on us for the rest of our lives, though it sometimes takes their absence for us to pay them the debt of memory and reflection. With increased discipline, focus, and commitment comes the feeling that life is taking me away from more people than it is taking me to—which to some extent is a matter of perspective—but also telling of a heart better acquainted with what it wants. It feels like one of those things falling into the category of quality over quantity, reminding myself to be grateful that something happened, rather than sad because it's over. Some might say we have but only so much love, and loving others helps us refine the love we eventually learn to give ourselves. This pilgrimage if you will—is often associated with loneliness and isolation—likely as key ingredients in our evolution and greater appreciation of

continued

continued

what is present. It's healthy to miss and be mindful of the people and places our paths have asked us to let go of, knowing in most cases, they could be revisited if we really wanted to. Angst from separation likely occurs because in many instances we are asked to make space and let things go, before we know who and what we are letting in. I guess that's why it's called sacrifice: It hurts a little, and all dreams, and all loves require it. In that regard, perhaps loneliness and isolation are good indicators that you've made more progress than you realize. Perhaps present angst is the yin to the yang of all of those intentions you planted into the earth. Maybe you needed to spend more time alone, to gain a greater understanding of just how much your time and presence are worth.

(debt of memory)

April 10th, morning snowfall
accumulation engulfs open water
stubborn and beautiful winter
teaching us to be patient for late spring
reaching for awe before the inconveniences it brings
listening to the birds when they sing
cracks in our disposition to let the light in
permission to go slow and find a grin
another opportunity to reach for gratitude
we control our effort, enthusiasm, and attitude
though we may tire from these platitudes
we do what we need, finding our way back to our feet
open to receive tests and blessings ahead
a day's rhythm begins before getting out of bed
so we practice prayer, meditation, and breath
striving to be present in this moment before the next
mindful how it feels when we give our best
and the way it hurts when we fail to
knowing we have some growing to do
trusting spring will arrive soon
remembering that like winter
we're stubborn and beautiful too
learning that like flowers
our time will come to bloom

(stubborn and beautiful)

Taking my time this time
gentler on my heart
easier on my mind
what I seek, I shall find
these hands weave magic
intertwining the divine
mused with ancient alchemy
fused with what love means to me
used by bones that break for me
guided by light shining so I can see
what we know of miracles
comes from what we believe
and what we learn to let go of
learning from and leaning in with love
discovering god is within, not above
remembering to walk before we run
knowing we're not for everyone
with great patience, great love comes
we were never meant to settle for crumbs
sometimes we're asked to fast before we feast
virtue cultivates curriculum, humanity needs
redwood trees grown from seeds
you will not hear a giant sequoia preach
stillness is the vehicle for the medicine
grace and time will teach

(ancient alchemy)

We don't always know
what we must let go
to set us free upon the path
rising above where we're at
healing from the past
climbing mountains to bask
in the sun after a great trek
yesterday's troubles
become but a speck
distanced and out of sight
tango at sunset with day and night
dancing on the precipice
of possibility and new beginnings
embracing the omnipresence
of darkness and light
being my purpose
as I write and type
the words and ways
that feel right
like song meeting sound
bare feet on ground
heart in the heavens
soul that leavens
wishes to willed
dreams to thrills
love that fills
and builds the unknown
into the people and places
we call home

(tango at sunset)

Sunshine and collective breath
community listens, and connects
better learning all the ways
to fill our days with love and grace
because hate is a goddamn waste
a symptom of suffering and fear
a spoiled child screaming for attention
obtuse and adverse to ascension
take a deep breath of oxygen
plant your feet on the earth
guide your heart to the stars
dreams are given to become ours
from sunrise to sunset
sunshine and collective breath
willing to listen, ready to connect
better aligning with our purpose
remembering that only love is worth it
because hate is a dangerous game
slowly seeping into your veins
taking root and planting shame
remember that each of us knows pain
and the frigidity of a cold, hard rain
so please take my words as my hand
feel their warmth as we begin to dance
because without love and hope in our hearts
none of us ever had a chance

(collective breath)

Some days just feel heavy: the coffee doesn't work; the excitement from publishing your first children's book doesn't land; and that only thing that sounds convincing is a nap. On these days I remind myself of something our friend John Lennon says, "Let it be." Growth and expansion take their energetic toll, and it feels like they're supposed to. Rest and reflection are essential tools in our evolution, and I'm thankful spring provides a vibrant backdrop for both. I will be retreating to a cabin in the woods tomorrow, and don't imagine it's a coincidence I'm feeling this way ahead of my time at Buhl Lake. Lately, I've been walking the trails in Addison Oaks in nearby Leonard, most recently to the tune of 30 miles in three days. It was on one of these walks a few weeks back when I discovered these rentable cabins in the woods. Closing in on another Mother's Day, and the anniversary of my mom passing, it is an especially emotional time for myself and so many others, who will be more viscerally navigating their grief these next few weeks. I continue to open myself to the ancient wisdom of nature, especially as it pertains to grief. Afterall, what mother has more experience with life, death, and letting go, than mother nature? Scientists discovered that the Earth has a

continued

continued

heartbeat: deep beneath our feet Earth emits a subtle, rhythmic pulse every 26 seconds. Known as the "microseismic", this barely detectable vibration originates from the ocean and travels through the planet like a soft heartbeat. Like most things it's there if and when we decide to listen. I've been creating a lot lately, and doing my best to embrace these energetic shifts as they come, and go. Living in a fast-paced world doesn't mean we have to be fast-paced, though it's the tendency. Birthing ideas, projects, and works of art require a great allotment of energy, making it not only logical but necessary that we rest, recoup, and retreat after their creation. Like most things society doesn't get quite right—it feels like we have the tendency to follow creation with a mad dash of tasks—because someone once said that's how to be successful. Somewhere in the back of my head is the all-telling voice speaking the cliche, "if you love something, set it free". I'll never be a mother, but art continues to teach me about loving, and letting go. When we're holding on too tight, there's little space for the unexpected. Being in the woods helps remind us of what is possible, and how little control we have on any of it.

(let it be)

May we be thankful for her waters
filling our cup and soothing our soul
reminding us to dance in the rain
shedding tears, shedding pain
loving those who gave us our names
knowing nothing will ever be the same
we've come too far to look back
weathered storms and remain intact
stronger for what didn't break us
kinder because of the places we let love take us
wiser for accepting all the things we do not know
more gentle after observing how nature
nurtures wild things to grow
readying us for the journey ahead
filling our bellies with grains grown into bread
calming the voices in our head
sleeping in and savoring the comfort of bed
camping in woods where flowers bloom
the warmth of a fire on a cool afternoon
receiving all that goodness, making its way to you
thankful for hearts that find a way to stay true
trusting there's no storm we won't find our way through
sky of blue, leaves of green
embrace the space of the unseen
after all, life is but a dream

(life is but a dream)

MY SUNSHINE

Sleeping with the windows open
waking to gentle rainfall on the lake
we learn to infuse sunshine in our own way
some of us meditate, some of us pray
others write books, while others bake
either way, life is sweeter when we create
trusting we go and grow at our own pace
graciously embracing stillness and change
despite our resistance we gather wisdom as we age
always finding a way to turn the page
willing our way forward with words
waking to the songs and sounds of birds
letting go of burdens because life and love hurt
we catch and release, because that is the work
wrinkled hands who have held their worth
kind eyes who have seen good people suffer
a hopeful heart who finds a way to keep hoping
an old soul does its best to remain open
a child plays without worry knowing
who or what they will one day be
or if they will ever measure up
because they already know they're enough
they already know they are love
infusing sunshine in their own way
going and growing at their own pace
reminding each of us
love's language is grace

(wrinkled hands)

May has felt more like fall this year
long sleeves and Americanos
cool breeze, windows open
fireside, wind blowing
making progress without knowing
where we're going or when we'll get there
grateful to be on our way
finding reasons to believe every day
protagonists in our own song
helping others belong
trusting that every feeling is fleeting
highs and lows blow with the wind
stay the course and let goodness in
let light and love lead the way
expect thunderstorms and a little rain
let your cathartic tears ease the pain
let yourself cry without the shame
it's alright if you're not okay
seasons and emotions come to pass
life is beautiful because it doesn't last
wind blows to let us know
we make progress without knowing
where we're going or when we'll get there
but change is in the air so keep your heart open
kind souls are worthy of everything they've been hoping

(a little rain)

Between thunderstorms and sunshine we flow
doing our best to remember growth is slow
choosing to believe the unexpected could be
better than anything we've yet to know
reminding ourselves to breathe easy and let go
embracing space made for good things to grow
making peace with the present and watering our soul
patience and consistency help our good parts show
thunderstorms and sunshine, darkness to light
riding a wave of the cosmos, under a star-filled night
children of the universe, charting our way home
learning from, loving, and helping one another
the quality of care we learn from mothers
the comfort of warmth we discover under covers
the softness of skin we learn from holding hands
the hue of blue we discover looking in someone's eyes
the serenity of a summer rain amidst dark skies
remembering what it feels like to belong in someone's arms
trusting there's time for our heart's desires to be ours
thunder and lightning, are darkness and light
feelings becoming words, and poetry as I type
fulfilling our heart's desires
to measure the quality of our lives
so here's to growing slow and taking notes
leading with your heart, and holding onto hope
between thunderstorms and sunshine we flow
being reminded to breathe easy and let go
thankful for all the space we made
for good things to grow

(growing slow & taking notes)

They say today—June 6 (6/6)—is deeply connected to harmony, love, home, balance, and nurturing energy. Numerologically, the number 6 is the "Mother" number. It's about community, emotional healing, and divine feminine energy. It comes as little surprise—though I'm only just now realizing this—today is also the two year anniversary of my mother's wake. We grew up on 6702 Windmill Lane; her family and friends gathered on 6/6 to mourn, pray, and share memories of her love; and on 6/7 we held her funeral and celebration of life. Our understanding of home is first, and in many instances forever shaped by our relationships with our mothers. They are the first arms we are held in, and the first place where we really belong. In the final years of her life my sense of home expanded, as her battle, and the pandemic helped me trust that we were meant to spend as much time together as we could—in the time she had left—on Hilton Head Island. Since the time of her passing I have prioritized healing, nurturing my gifts, and building a better balance between home and the road. Hilton Head will always be home in its own way, but Michigan is the community where I lay roots. It is the place—I think— she would want me to be, to receive the very blessings and love I have grown and gardened. Today, each of us is invited to reconnect with our

continued

continued

inner selves, purpose, and those parts of us that may have been lost, or forgotten. It is a chance to rewrite one's life with a renewed intention and purpose. We honor our mothers by beginning again anew, and making space for the version of ourselves that we love the most. Reflect, release, rebuild. Make peace within, so it may be revealed in your perception of the world. The divine feminine calls us to direct our gaze inward, clear blocks, and plant powerful intentions during this time of amplified vibration. In other words: it's a good day to love yourself in all the ways you may have been missing or neglecting; and it's a good day to take an honest look at the way your life's been going, and ask yourself if you want to spend the next six months or six years going in the same direction? Either way, you have permission to greet and treat yourself with kindness, patience, and grace—because that's what our mothers would have done.

(what our mothers would have done)

Tired and resting. Loving and trusting. Finding my way back to my flow and feel. These intuitions have always been real. This heart has always been an engine. One of these days, comes love worth mentioning. Holding on by letting go. Maintaining space for my good parts to show. Look how much we've better balanced home and the road. Imagine all the ways our words have shaped others' lives, and helped them grow. I bet you'd be more gentle with yourself if you were given even a glimpse of the difference you've made. Your life is a living, breathing, testimony of what it takes. Your journey is evidence that we grow stronger and rise after we break. Love has taught you to forgive and not forsake. Abundance blesses those who give more than they take. You learned to trust the part of you that always knew you were great. With kindness and intention, our better world is made. One day at a time, or you might go insane. Plenty of laughter and leisure, or you'll grow lame. Your name means something to someone, and that's a pretty cool thing. Someone thinks about you when they sing. Someone thanks you for showing them how to better let love in. Someone is quietly cheering for you to win. Someone tells stories about you to their children to help them feel better. Someone wouldn't be here if it wasn't for you. Someone, somewhere marvels at how much you've grown.

continued

continued

Someone, somewhere thinks of you and feels home. This heart has always been an engine. Fueled by abundant love, worth mentioning. Holding on by letting go. Grateful for space and time, where these hands and heartbeat help my best art grow. Creating something today that may comfort and guide tomorrow. If it is love you need please reach out, and I'll offer what I'm able for you to borrow.

(engine)

We have the tendency to be harder on ourselves when we are sick or injured—even though it's plain to see that when we are ill or hurting—we need more love not less. Everything is a little harder when you're in pain, and being kind to yourself just so happens to be another one of those things. Where does this social tendency come from to kick a man when he is down? Why have we allowed ourselves to be conditioned into taking cheap shots when one's defenses are down? I imagine it stems from our relationship with ourselves, and the tone of the internal conversation we carry while navigating turbulence. Words are wands, weaving ways of wonder or worry. Be mindful of the words you choose when speaking to yourself, especially when you're hurting. Like Otis Redding says, "Try a Little Tenderness", and offer yourself some of that grace you're so quick to and good at offering others. No matter what ails you, rest is likely an essential ingredient in your journey towards relief. Give yourself the same reasonable accommodations you would offer your children, parents, siblings, friends, or lover, without the cheap shots. Remember, that sometimes we are being slowed down for a reason, as a courtesy, to make space and better prepare us for what's to come. We are neither machines nor mundane, but a departure from wellness can make us feel

continued

continued

broken down and faulty, while dulling our usual sense of passion and purpose. It's alright to feel this way— just try to identify when you are— and let a little tenderness into the narrative you are having with yourself. Not every day was meant for climbing mountains. Some days are meant to be exactly where you are, helping you learn to love yourself when it's a little harder, because you need it that much more. Being kind to others begins with being kind to ourselves, especially on the days when it's hard. Sickness, injury, and pain can be the cracks through which we learn to let a little more light and love in—but for now— just try to offer yourself some of the patience and relief you know you need today.

(try a little tenderness)

July. Summer. Shooting stars. Northern Lights. Motown music. The 4th. The Lake. Up North. Concerts in the park. Golden Retrievers. Baseball. Sunsets. Ice cream. Camping. Sun-kissed skin. Late nights. Long kisses. Sleepovers. Wine strolls. Beach days. Messy hair. Family reunions. Pizza delivery. River floats. Projector movies. Iced coffee. Music festivals. Bon fires. Tigers games. Pure Michigan. A collective breath as we reach the half way point in a year filled with growth, lunacy, astonishment, war, highs, lows, and a big batch of being human. Humanity is human. Not always our best, not always our worst. Most days we fall somewhere in between the person we hope to be, and the person we were. Progress is messy and impatient, hurried and ignorant. We hope for more than we work for, or work for more than we hope for. We want the best, and pack a parachute to prepare for the worst. But guess what? Most of us are trying to rise, and help those along our sides to do the same. We don't get to choose which wars our nation fights, but we get to choose the people who do— and we're learning the price of making choices based on fear, scarcity, and ignorance. We don't get to choose who our neighbors are, or how they behave, but all on our own we have the choice to be kind, decent humans who treat others how we'd like to be treated. We have the ability to let our ethics,

continued

continued

behavior, and outward inertia of our heart's love in the world paint a picture of the type of community we hope to live in. When we start consistently showing up for one another you'd be astonished at how many of our troubles went away. When we show up for ourselves, showing up for others is revealed as the logical next step. It's been a period of great learning, growth, expansion, and revelation. Once we steadily operate from a place of love, it becomes painfully obvious who isn't. It isn't our job to make them, shame them, or blame them, but to let them go and walk away. Everyday we get to make the choice to operate from love or fear, and it's a choice we must make over and over again, or have it made for us. After a while, it stops feeling like a choice. Goodness becomes you like stars shine in the night sky. Stars don't choose to shine, rather, it's what they are. Each of us is meant to shine as a means to help another find its place in a world where darkness tangoes with light. Just keep trying and before long you'll find your place in the night sky, surrounded by the stars who help you shine.

(light of mine)

Who am I? How is it that I love? Why is it that I love? How did I come to learn about what it is to love? I am a witness of experience, emotion, energy, evolution, and emergence. I am aware that certain experiences, certain people, and certain environments make me feel a certain way, in an uncertain world. I understand that empathy is my ability to consider these phenomena from a perspective beyond my own. I've learned that the way something or someone makes me feel is the most genuine and effective means of evaluating my relationship with it. I've learned that I am a balance of the love given to me by the relationships I inherited, the love I give to myself, the love I give to others, and the love I allow myself to receive. I am more than a finite set of experiences occurring in my 40 years of consciousness, given the opportunity to remember what I do not know. Some days it feels like I've forgotten more than I've remembered. Most days I know that it doesn't matter. Most days are better when elevated with intention. The sweet nectar of knowingly choosing in a realm that loves to choose for you. Fitting in, by standing out. Utilizing the obvious, in excellence. Being radial, in love. Patient, in process. Grateful for recess. A friend of success. Recognize excess. Expect less, while leaving the door open for more. My love is my life's work and I don't

continued

continued

speak it lightly, yet give it freely. Blue skies, and cumulonimbus clouds are a poet's ceiling. Only emerging galaxies and the stars will be the indicators if we've traveled too far, in discovery of what was always ours. Our love is made of life, death, and scars; our skin marked at birth with the stain of red wine and mars. We are what we know and trust ourselves to be—keys that belong to no locks—still opening doors to help others be free. The wear and tear of our pages is where the love seeps in as our story ages; porous to a chorus of harmony and healing, growing in love by following this feeling.

(worn pages)

We gather to remember present blessings in our life. We rest to celebrate the distances our journey has taken us. We give thanks knowing that our time together is fleeting. We use our hands and heart to show others that they are not alone. We use our words with hopes that others might understand how we feel, and what it means to live our lives with or without them in it. We spend our time with people in places who become the characters and setting in the story of our lives. We hope that the love we give others will find its way into a warmer, softer world. We pray that the ones we love will look to and lean on us in their time of need. We learn that asking for help is a divine form of trust. We understand that needing help isn't a form of weakness. We discover strength in places we once perceived as weak. We use our strengths to help others in their time of need. We help because we're able. We're often able because someone helped. We are in this together. We are better together. We are not at war with anyone other than ourselves. We cannot defeat ourselves. War has no victors, only victims. Let us gather to remember present blessings in our life. Let us rest to celebrate the distance our journey has taken us. Let us give thanks knowing that our time together is fleeting. Let us use our hands and heart to show others that they are not alone. Let us use our words to help lift

continued

continued

others when the weight is too great to carry. Let us spend time with people in places who make our life's story worth telling. Let us freely give our love knowing we live in a warmer, softer world because of it. Let us bury our burdens and set them free—grace and abundance crave peace—the very way forests flower from trees and seeds. Love is all around us, because it is us, and one of these days we'll just have to believe.

(one of these days)

If this guitar could sing
it would thank the trees for bringing it to life
making music for the same reason stars shine at night
finding purpose in service of those fighting the good fight
an aid to slay those who aim to deny rights
a reminder when decency strays too far from sight
an osmosis of sound, harmony, love, and light
a wave of the cosmos, and tumbling dice
fate forged by faith, fear, fire, & ice
trying our best not to think twice
grains of sand, song, salt, & rice
grateful the earth gave us life
making music to accompany stars shining at night
finding purpose in service of those fighting the good fight
an aid to slay those who deny rights
a reminder of better days in sight
an osmosis of sound, harmony, love, and light
a wave of the cosmos, and tumbling dice
singing songs accompanied by trees given life
divine instruments, shaped by hearts, hands, time, & knives
raising vibrations, raising the tides
where do chaos and chorus finally collide?
isn't it time we align with our ingredients inside?
made from love above, and the earth below
music moves, water falls, rivers flow

(if this guitar could sing)

Wounds and fear live deep
when we don't let them go, pain seeps
their heaviness lingers until we release
opening our hearts to inner peace
making space for the coming feast
we practice and prepare for what's coming next
but what do we know of what we cannot expect?
limits will lean on you and try to harden
growth softens the soil in our garden
pardoning us from pain
welcoming the rain
letting go of shame
tending to our flame
breathing deeper when it wanes
patience when it flickers
we learn to trust our shivers
pure connection to source
guiding soul's intended course
true north means looking up
ascension requires love
heightened blessings reside above
you've carried what's heavy far enough
let go and dare to see
what awaits you to be free

(far enough)

Love, life, and our gifts are often measured by who we share them with. Please remember that you're someone too; worthy and deserving of every ounce of sunshine dancing upon your skin. Engulfed within a world screaming for attention, we must embrace the solitude we need to flourish. Managing other people's needs and expectations is exhausting, especially when it comes at the expense of our own. Thankfully, every day we have the choice to give ourselves what we need—without abandoning our commitments to others. Like most things in life it just takes practice, patience, and grace. We have the tendency to neglect and or scapegoat inner work (practice), claiming our *responsibilities* are keeping us from the rituals and routines we intend to implement. I've said it before and I will say it again—a well without water wills no wishes—and if your well-being isn't considered within your *responsibilities*, you're doing it wrong. My glimpses of the internet reveal chaos, set on a course to tumble from the top down. A series of people, institutions, and archaic dispositions which refuse to get out of their own way, causing harm and hurt to others while ships take on water, in stormy seas. While I understand that the answer isn't to look away, my heart tells me to look less. We have the unique opportunity to control our gaze, and choose who and what we

continued

continued

give our attention to. The news will rarely give you answers, and nature will always nurture. Made of water and stardust, the universe within is more vast than the galaxies without. Make time and take time to explore your wonder within. Nobody knows what you need more than yourself, but each of us needs a reminder to better listen. I want you to be happy. I want you to be healthy. I want you to be safe. I want you to be at ease. I want these things for you, because I *need* them for me. Please give yourself whatever permission you need to find the routines which bring you peace. If, and when you find yourself saying prayers for others, try to remember to say at least one for yourself. You don't have to look away, but the real journey begins with our commitment to look within.

(water & stardust)

Stars above, earth below
magic abound when we flow
observe your thoughts and let them go
seeds need change to grow
it's come time we start looking up
stifled by fear, lifted in love
hope sings for all living things
born beneath the stars, in a mother's arms
protected by ancestors who have come to pass
guided by something that isn't yours to take away
humbled by the journey, loss, and pain
honoring life by asking others to do the same
begging for reason, when governance is vain
lending courage to help others dance in the rain
empathy for those weathered by the storm
acknowledgement that history repeats itself
wisdom that it doesn't have to
trust that there's a better way
willingness to be seeds of change
learning from and transcending pain
harmonizing hopeful songs for all living things
born beneath the stars, in a mother's arms
breath is birthright on our journey
to remember who we are
and what we could be
once we begin to believe

(in a mother's arms)

We are a rising tide comprised of old souls, shooting stars, and hungry hearts. An underdog story fueled by empathy, forged in fire, and written in love. We have been battered and we have been broken, only to discover the strength awoken from such depths. The world has shattered our armor, helping us discover that cracks are where the light comes in. Our ships have been swallowed by raging seas in the dead of night, teaching us how to tread water just long enough to be saved by rescue boats in the coming dawn. They told us to have dreams so we held them in our hearts long enough to learn how beautiful and terrifying that it can be, to carry something you love that much. We are a testament of endurance, a deep ocean current, carrying the best of yesterday into the imagination of tomorrow. A reminder that you will never have to do it alone, because each of us understands what it feels like to carry a weight too great to bear. We are the courage to be a voice of compassion and reason, while tyranny and apathy starve children in the streets. Whether we know it or not, each of us is being called to rise. There comes a time in our lives where we must be more, if we want more. Sunday sermons will not do the work on your behalf. Spirit moves each of us in direct proportion to our willingness and capacity to be moved. What words does your heart whisper to you in the rare, quiet

continued

continued

moments where you're willing to listen? What love have you denied yourself and others as a result of pain you're not ready to face? When will be the right time for you to heal, let go, and grow? Ancient wisdom flows through your veins; an infinite inertia patiently waiting for you to take the reins and set your potential free. We are darkness, we are light, souls on a temporary human flight. We are war, we are peace, we are hungry children in the streets. A rising tide comprised of old souls, shooting stars, and hungry hearts. An underdog story fueled by empathy, forged in fire, and written in love. Heaven above, hell below; if you never try, you'll never know.

(hungry hearts)

The best is yet to come. You haven't lived the best days of your life yet. You're not alone. You're not naive for seeing the best in people. You're not foolish to believe in basic human rights. More of us are like you than you may think. Most of us are hard on ourselves. Most of us could be kinder to ourselves. Most of us are a work in progress. Most of us have compromised our dreams in one way or another. Each of us has the opportunity to begin again. Most things don't last. Your perspective determines whether that is a blessing or a burden. Your heart knows what it wants, and your joy indicates that you are walking in the right direction. Your choices can reflect your understanding of the latter. Your days can be filled how you choose. Your time can be spent doing what you love. Your inner circle doesn't have to include people who dim your light. Your work doesn't have to crush your soul. Some of your "have to's" are likely comfort zones. Opening your heart and mind helps welcome subtle changes with the potential to move mountains. You can ask for what you need. You have permission to believe in yourself and *irrational dreams*. And here's another secret: you can give others permission to believe in theirs. There are little ways to simplify your life. You've probably already figured a few of them out. Your life is a work of art. Your attitude is a choice.

continued

continued

You've created more good in the world than you give yourself credit for. You owe yourself a few apologies for the way you speak to yourself. Turns out, it's a lot easier to forgive ourselves if we try. Life, love, learning, and fun can be messy. Nature is wild. Thunderstorms release pent up energy. Rain cleanses. Accidents happen. Pain passes. Love builds, breaks, and mends. People who make you feel home are family. There will always be places you belong. There will always be people you outgrow. Smile because it happened. Remember when you need to. Let go if it is time. Let the love you've been asking for in. Learn from children and animals. Be silly where the opportunity emerges. Be silly even if it doesn't. Be proud without thinking you need to be loud. Be kind without needing it in return. Be yourself by learning who that is. Be love by learning what it takes. Be an ally by understanding how much it could mean. Be the vision of yourself that reflects the accumulation of moments and choices which flowed naturally. Be what you need to be, when you need to be it, and own it without explanation.

(build, break, & mend)

It's a bit odd how the most ignorant people are the most enthusiastic, and frequent to tell others what America is. It feels like a lot of people with hate in their heart who refuse to think for themselves, read a book, or acknowledge the elephant in the room. I'm 40-years-old and I grew up learning that America is the melting pot of the world. A place where everyone has a chance, where equality matters, and anything is possible with hard work and a dream. I learned that we stand up for the little guy, cheer for the underdog, and sacrifice for what we love. I was taught that our differences are a source of strength, helping is human, and respect is earned. My grandparents fled Lithuania following World War II—escaping the Iron Curtain—eventually starting a new life in America. How many of your parents and grandparents have similar stories? When did we let immigrant become a bad word? Why did we start embracing ignorance as a lens through which we see the world? One cannot grasp what being American is, without understanding where our roots reside. We are a people made up of displaced people, who endured great hardship in pursuit of something better. Why is it that these days we seem so intent to settle for something worse? In 1967 The Beatles released "All You Need Is Love"—and despite our technological advances—58 years later we continue to let human decency fall through our fingertips. We've allowed celebrity culture to occupy a piece of the pie where reason, ethics, and love once held their place. We've allowed law to be determined by those who refuse to operate within its sanctity. We have watched the office of the president turn into a bad, and predictable country music song. As

continued

continued

frustrating as this continues to be, it's a reflection of our priorities as a people. It's a symptom of being unwell, stemming from lives hungry for love, purpose, and joy. It is so much easier to blame others, than be accountable. We have freely traded care for convenience, kindness for station, and cause for comfort. We the people will not be defined by the actions of a select few; but we damned well better be concerned with what our modern political climate says about this way of life we've grown accustomed to. Be so bold that you dare to learn someone's story before condemning them with your judgement. Have the courage to work on some of your own problems before kicking another while they're down; or better yet, help them back up. America, we've reached the part of the story where we have an opportunity for character development. We are better than this and most of you either know it in your hearts, or hope for it on the horizon. If you remember who you are, and where you come from, it shouldn't be so hard to see the parts that don't belong. It's never too late to rewrite your story with a little more kindness and love. America, you are still beautiful—even while you're having an identity crisis.

(america, the beautiful?)

How many things were impossible until someone proved otherwise? How many causes were lost until a protagonist emerged and helped find a way? Adversity breeds character, and sometimes down-and-out is where the fun begins. Great stories require conflict, and persistence finds a way. The climb elevates the view, and the descent happens twice as fast. Life isn't a scavenger hunt requiring us to check the appropriate number of boxes, so we can say we played the game right. Life is what you want it to be, and what you're willing to discover and sacrifice along the way to make it so. Experience is knowledge, and the accumulation of knowledge expands our perception of this human experiment. Learning helps lift ourselves and others, and ought not be used to hold another down. Loving invites empathy into our hearts, teaching us to hold on when we have to, and let go when we must. Caring about others helps us better care for ourselves. Pain encourages growth. Growth processes pain. Grief interprets loss. Loss heightens your clarity of what is meaningful. What is meaningful changes form, but always remains. Today is a reflection of yesterday, but not determined by it. Tomorrow is a reflection of today, but not limited by it. You are not your choices but your choices reflect what you care about. What you care about will naturally change over time. It's never too

continued

continued

late to try again. You are not the same person as you were then. The world is not the same place as it was then. If you're waiting for the right time, there won't be one. If you're waiting on someone, you'll always be. If you need help, ask for it. If you don't believe in it, find something that you do. Once you've bled for something, it changes you. Hunger is a powerful force. Dreams don't need to be forced—but if you hear it calling—stay the course. Impossible is a limited perspective. Lost causes are waiting to be found. Pages beg to be written. You're given dreams for a reason. Somewhere they've already come true. The divine expresses itself through you. God sees through your eyes. Love grows with the beat of your heart. You are the hero of this story. Only you can decide what is worth saving. Only you can decide to keep going. Only you can find what you're looking for. And only you know what it's supposed to feel like when you've found it.

(waiting to be found)

Revolution begins within. Small, intentional, and consistent choices transform our inner world until eventually they take root, sprouting visible change in the environments we operate in. Empowered people have both the capacity and tendency to use their gifts to help lift others up. It's difficult to show up for others, when we're experiencing difficulty showing up for ourselves. With that said, you'd be amazed at all the little ways you can begin to show up for yourself. It's a journey made one choice and direction at a time. It often begins with slowing down, and taking the time to listen to some things you've been trying to tell yourself for a while. Maybe let your guard down some, and be curious in the places where you're defensive. It's funny how growth scares us, even though it's the very device which delivers our dreams and prayers. If something means enough for you to consistently ask for it, anything that brings it closer to you seems worth exploring. Commitment and fortitude are the asking price of dreams. To want something so much, and believe in it long enough that the only way out is through. We are magnetic beings, capable of moving heaven and earth with our continual choice to do so. You don't have to seek greatness to recognize, and acknowledge it within. Beauty is not bound by a single path. We learn more about ourselves when we get lost. The way is

continued

continued

never out of reach. Your thoughts are the harshest reality. Your kindness is the key. Your happiness asks for balance. Your joy asks for your attention. Your priorities think you should be one of them. Your dreams require courage. Your love is fuel. Revolution begins within. To truly love others we must better love ourselves. Our time here is meaningful, and we have the unique ability to decide how we spend it. The world needs what you need. You can't help others while you're drowning. Embrace the life rafts you have access to, retreat, regroup, and try again when you have the capacity to carry on. Your struggle makes you human, and is no cause for shame. What would we know of sunshine without a little rain? Great wisdom resides within a little pain. Start choosing yourself and you'll never be the same. Listen to that heart of yours, calling your name. Rise, and reach for your stars by first accepting that it's okay to be right where you are.

(the asking price of dreams)

Where I've been ain't where I'm goin', but it will help me find the way as it's revealed. Wading in the water and listening to the wind—we discover magic with the choice to begin—then one day understand what it means to be all in. If there is a time for all things, I sure hope you make time for the ingredients that make your soul sing. You don't have to be good at math to concoct an equation you'd like to see last. You don't have to know where a journey will take you, to know it is time to take it. If you love something you shouldn't ever have to fake it. If your current reality doesn't meet the vision in your heart, what are you willing to do to make it? Summer is a place in my heart that will never fade. The season where dreams are set free to run, play, and create. From baseball diamonds to concerts, coffee shops, and the lakes; swooned by 9pm sunsets, endless pages, and summer days. I haven't written my life's story yet, because I'm actively living it. I've never held back my heart, because I discovered who I am by giving it. Passion, patience, persistence, and peace: a dreamer's guidebook for everything he needs. Of course it isn't easy but what meaningful thing in your life is? Make a wish and will it. Write yourself a prescription and fill it. Hold something beautiful in your heart and build it. August reminds us to be wild and at play, calm and courageous, until we

continued

continued

remember what we came here to say. Major Tom to ground control, musical dreams and rock'n roll. Singing softly and sweetly so we know you can feel it; find your reasons to believe and don't reveal it. We carry and covet something until we love it. One day we will rise above it and keep looking up, but if it doesn't hurt a little it probably isn't love. Set your sights on the stars but don't overlook the flowers below. You can love who you are today, while acknowledging space to grow. Worn hands know how to row. Dream weavers learn how to sew. Walk in the direction you want to go, until it is time to run. Your higher calling isn't meant for everyone. When it starts to get hard, know it could be about to get fun. When it gets too heavy, ask for help. When you fall down, get back up. Take your time, what's the rush? Honor your true colors, wear your blush; paint your dreams, with each stroke of the brush.

(a dreamer's guidebook)

How I welcome September's cool and crisp embrace; returning home, returning to myself, and my good habits. Sleeping alongside the lake, windows open, heart ready for all that belongs to stay. The trio of gals continue to practice their morning swim across the lake. My fingers thank me for their return to turning paper pages, so the rest of me may absorb their wisdom in the places which ache. The words of others help the cathartic release of my tears, comforting me like the warm, flannel blanket which lays upon my legs. My internal peace continues to paint the landscape of my external horizon, forever grateful for the abundance and harmony which accompany it. I have become more than I was yesterday, by letting go of what was never mine to begin with. I have made new friends who feel like family, on the peninsula which calls me home. When they go to Japan in October, I will live in their Tiny Home with their Aussiedoodles Appa and Gromit, slumbering aside West Bay and trees with technicolor leaves. Each of us is called in the direction of our dreams—when we listen and align with that calling—spirit moves us with cadence and care. There is a divine whisper betwixt and between all things that becomes a roar, when we remember to see the forest for the trees. In the presence of certain people and places our guitars are more vibrantly tuned, urging us to

continued

continued

frequent and keep the company of those which more consistently invite us to reach for our stars. Reaching isn't chasing, and gratitude is embracing. Silent sounds and wonders sing for your comfort and joy, laying the tracks upon your journey home. Dreams come true because they're the best parts of you, fighting their way to the forefront, celebrating that you're different. Forest felt like running, some feel like strumming—what buried treasures have you been shunning? We are pushed and pulled by ancient wisdom, isn't it logical that we allow ourselves to be moved by divine vision? Summer fades into a blazing autumn night, inviting us inward to everything we know feels right. Let go of chaos and clutter, offering yourself the love and kindness you'd give another. There comes a time to hold on and a time to leave, wisdom is trusting the timing you need. Trees teach us that it is easier to change colors than it is to change hearts—but we must let go of what refuses to grow—if we hope to change ours.

(forest for the trees)

Tell yourself the words you hope others say to you. Don't wait for someone else to tell you when the timing is right. Trust that Universal Flow will show you where you belong. Listen long enough to hear what you need to. Recognize turbulence as a divine path to triumph. Treasure silence. Try something different. Make a difference. Try to understand that the voice in your head is fear more than it is truth. Consider that breakthroughs await on the other side. Helping others is divine. Life should be a good time. Reading a good book is a great way to unwind. Most heavy things get lighter in time. You get to decide what is a good sign. Our plans pale in comparison to the architecture of spirit's design. I hope you're coming to terms with how rare you are of a find. I hope you're learning that gifts are meant to be shared. I hope you no longer fault yourself for that generous heart of yours, and all of the times it hurts because you care. I feel by now you're beginning to trust that you're meant for something bigger. Try not to be discouraged when it doesn't happen the way you think. Try not to doubt yourself when it takes longer than you hoped. Remember what the climb taught you if you're asked to begin again. Recognize those on a similar journey. Treasure the bond that it creates between you. Lean on it when you're feeling low. Creation is connection. Connection is intention.

continued

continued

Intention is ascension. Ascension is divine. Ground your feet and reach for the stars. Feel their presence within you. Recognize the best parts of yourself in others. Different but the same. Many reflections, many names. Guided in the directions that call us. Moved by the water within us. Echoing the harmonies that sing to us. Breathing the air that teaches us. Honoring the bodies that hold us. Grateful for the love that comes to us. Embracing the strength of gentle touch. Making time, offering trust. Miracles born from love and dust. Telling others the words they need to hear. Helping others trust that the timing is right. Reminding others that there will always be places they belong. We are the river, we are the road—honoring creation—by carrying it where it flows.

(we are the river)

Take a few moments to consider how far you've come. Without cause or concern for tomorrow, relish in the seemingly infinite number of yesterdays that helped teach you to be the force of nature who arrived here today. How many troubles never came? How many blessings always found a way to? Why do you think that is? Surely you're beginning to accept that you're the common denominator, faith is a friend, and you always find a way. We have the tendency to become the conversations we carry, reminding us to declutter our thoughts the very way we need to filter out the noise of our external environments. We are under no obligation to grant others a platform within our narrative on the subject of what is meaningful, necessary, and true. Wisdom isn't measured in decibels, clicks, follows, or views. Being there for someone doesn't mean exclusively at their convenience. You can hear what someone has to say without identifying it as advice. You can lend your empathy without offering your storage capacity to carry another's weight. Our personal journey brings us to and away from people for a reason; trust that there is a season for learning, and a season for leaving. All along you alone have possessed the permission to listen to your heart, trust its guidance—while learning from, and letting go of its resistance. How many chances have you had to take just to be

continued

continued

where you are today? How many people would have done it differently if given the chance? You have captained the ship thus far—navigating the cosmos—trust that you are the only one capable of authoring your continued ascent. Storms will approach, rage, dissipate, and every time you will remain. We emerge on the other side when we choose to—changed for the better—because blue skies are sweeter after a little thunder. Today is evidence of the abundance in your tomorrow. When you win, everybody wins. Your journey matters and will continue to. Your hard work, patience, and kindness deliver you. The common denominator, who never lets good wait for later. Standing in the arena—holding your ground—transcending the clamor of spectators. Rising to the occasion, embracing inherited station; being decent while surfing the waves of creation.

(the common denominator)

I try to write something great every day because life is sweeter when I do. It doesn't always come to fruition, but accepting that I want it helps me commit to it. Our commitments ought to in some sense reflect what we want. I understand that's not always the immediate case, but if you're not building towards what you want, what is it that you're doing? Each of us owes a debt to ourselves to live a life we enjoy that is fulfilling and true to our nature. When we identify and engage in such activities, we discover the humbling nature of the process, while gaining a greater appreciation for all those skilled in the art of alchemy. Life requires life; as such, we must give a piece of ourselves to the very dreams we wish to bring forth. As a result, intuition leads us in the direction of experiences that are worth the sacrifice. It is logical that we offer our time, energy, and love to people, activities, and commitments which align with our hearts, resonate with our soul, and ultimately help us gain ground on what we want in our lives. This isn't to say that each act must be a stepping stone in an infinite series of calculations en route to achieve our dreams, rather a reminder that you have both the freedom and responsibility to pursue whatever version of intention and excellence you desire for your life. Commitment requires discipline, and

continued

continued

discipline helps teach us to honor service. Each of us is better learning to serve ourselves, while letting go of a lifetime of bad advice telling us to honor and pursue an external, ideological dream. Composed of infinite intricacy and nuance, your recipe for fulfillment and success should be similarly unique and reflect those subtle yet profound qualities. Go your own way. Don't follow a flight plan from someone who has never left the ground. Trust your internal compass more than the advice of a stranger. Learn what you love by listening to your heart and leaning in. Take a chance on yourself by committing to something you love. Know that the journey will teach you more than any perceived failure could take away. Give yourself to something you want, and let it lead you to something or someone you love.

(internal compass)

You know what fits versus what is forced. You know the difference between what you want, and what you're told to want. You can sense who has your back, opposed to those who only pretend to. You know what lights you up, and what makes you cringe. Knowing one's self is a continual exploration, navigated with questions, observations, and adjustments. It asks for our patience, trust, and honesty as our intuition guides us to the people and places who and where we're meant to be. Our willingness to listen enhances our ability to hear. The wind whispers truths only our hearts can interpret. Flowing and feeling are instruments of a similar tune. Guidance is embedded in preference. Observe the way something makes you feel, and listen to the emotions it does or doesn't reveal. Vibrations are very real. Synchronicities appear along the way. People can be obstacles, and people can be guides; over time you'll see it with your own eyes. Trust what you see. Be who you know yourself to be. They do not know what you are capable of, but maybe it's time for you to learn. Rivers run without being in a hurry. Growth is the willingness to keep learning. Finally facing those fears you keep burying. Emotion is meant to be felt, not carried. Catharsis releases what is scary. Let go of what's heavy, and embrace what is light. Move freely and fluidly like the water

continued

continued

you are. You are not defined, rather made beautiful by your scars. Our blemishes tell a story. Our pain asks us to grow. Our grief teaches us how to better love. Our hearts know it's possible. Our hands do the work. Our love teaches us to be tenacious. Our tenacity requires endurance. Endurance teaches us when to rest. Resting is a form of healing. Healing happens when we listen. Flowers grow with water and sunlight. Ascension occurs when we trust what feels right. Flowing and feeling are instruments of a similar tune. When your heart makes demands, trust them to be true. When the music speaks to you, allow yourself to be moved. What is meant for you, will not require duct tape and gorilla glue.

(water and sunlight)

We grow more aware of our sharp edges, learning to soften them by seeing them. We are conditioned by so many people, places, and events before we even learn what it means to be. We don't know what we don't know, thankfully experience comes along to guide us toward what we came here to learn. Sometimes this means traveling to a place we've never been, renting a house near a Great Lake, and letting the first day of autumn arrive in whatever way it's meant to. Today it means finishing a good book on a blanket at the beach in Sleeper State Park, a swim in the blue waters of Lake Huron, and a late afternoon fire ahead of watching the Lions on Monday Night Football. I've been working more than usual lately which made it easy to let myself be drawn to the Thumb to relax, release, and experience something for the first time. Mondays are quiet in Caseville at this junction of the year, and right now I appreciate quiet. It is once again time for me to go inward—shifting with the seasons—making space and time to reflect and treasure what has come to pass. Are blessings dampened when we fail to fully appreciate them? Is growth overlooked and stifled if we've already moved on to the next climb? Where is there proof that hurrying for tomorrow, makes anything better today? Yesterday felt like summer, and today feels like fall. The birds continue to sing, the leaves are

continued

continued

changing colors, and we sleep with the windows open. Most days (if we're lucky) feel like some combination of an Iron & Wine and Caamp song. We gather fireside, prepare for harvest, and look each other in the eyes. It's a wondrous time to embrace each breath, savoring these crispy days before winter coming next. Cooler mornings and cooler nights, thunderstorms and northern lights. Comforted and guided by trees and forests, welcoming change, and letting go of what isn't for us. Our willingness to go where we haven't, improves the likelihood of receiving what we've asked for. Relish in the breath between seasons, and trust that if you hold it in your heart there's a reason. May we each travel to places we've never been, by first offering our gratitude for all of those that we have.

(the places we've never been)

You can only be you, and your best is all that you can do. Some days are thunder, some days are lightning, and some days it just fucking pours. Storms will come and storms will go, sunshine will dance upon your skin and feel like home. Highs will be followed by lows, and your life will mostly be lived somewhere in-between. Why not enjoy it no matter what? Why not try and learn what it feels like to lead with love? Turn off the news and throw away postcards from hell. Let fools keep the company of fools and walk away. I'm not walking away from you, I'm just walking towards *everything* else. I did not come here to tolerate or carry your hate. Education is liberation. Kindness is the cure. Helping hands pick up the broken pieces. Tenacity finds a way. Combating evil requires faith, but prayers will not suffice. Show up for yourself so one day soon you will know what it is to show up for others. Give yourself a chance at being something great, by no one's definition but your own. Isn't it time to listen to that precious and beautiful heart of yours? Isn't it time to call a spade a spade, and disarm the elephant in the room? What are we protecting when it doesn't feel safe for a mother to send her child to school? What do we call sacred when lives are taken in spiritual sanctuaries? What promise have we been so gullible to believe that accumulating more wealth will make us

continued

continued

feel any more safe tomorrow than we are today? How is anyone's relationship with their weapon of greater sanctity than their relationship with their child, or family? How do we still seek shelter from tornadoes in this house of cards? We are failing each other by failing ourselves. Misery is a dangerous disease. Hate is weakness personified. Life is sacred, perhaps we should act as such. Ignorance is the fan, our unwillingness is the flame. Empathy asks that we try things a different way. Children point fingers and scapegoat blame. They eventually know better. We know better. What is the place of knowledge if met with apathy? Without integrity and compassion, your freedom is an illusion. Hate and distaste poison the wells they live in. Violence is weakness. Evidence of a faulty foundation. Proof of system failure. A cry for help. The embodiment of a failed American dream. A reason to consider things from a different perspective. A plea for each of us to be better. A reason to grow every day, no matter the weather. Some days are thunder, some days are lightning, and some days it just fucking pours. A lot of good people are giving their best most days, maybe it's time to give yours.

(when it rains it pours)

Sometimes our bodies ask us to slow down, other times it screams. I believe the energy of each season builds until it can be released with the arrival of the next. For the first time in my life I've experienced tension headaches. It's been over two weeks and while I'm not out of the woods yet, I'm consistently sleeping better, and feeling the peace that comes from carrying less. Knowing I'd spend most of October and November on the Leelanau, I ended another concert season in a sprint for the finish. We find our limits by way of the scientific method, learning to be softer on ourselves while we discover new boundaries. We expand and we contract. We push, flow, pick up speed, and rest. Grace is the ever growing familiarity with one's boundaries, and the understanding that some things are meant to be managed, while others ask to be let go of. I haven't been writing lately because it's difficult to focus when I'm in pain, and looking at a screen rarely makes anything feel any better. Even now I feel the energy and sound of the room encroaching—while I type these words from Fiddleheads in Lake Leelanau—finding my way back to myself after a hearty breakfast. During times of internal and external unrest, it's important that we remember to look to nature, spend time amongst the trees, and observe to absorb the beauty of metamorphosis, and the wisdom of frailty. As

continued

continued

each of us learns to better listen to our god given, cosmic calling, intuition—we discover tangible ways to show up for others while embracing the space we need to heal. It's important to trust that the universe rarely gives you more than you can handle, so try your best to be open to receive lessons and blessings while navigating turbulence. It is no coincidence that I've been met with these headaches where and when I'm in the space and time to observe them, listen to what they're saying, and rest as needed. I'm six days into my aussiedoole adventure, living with Appa and Gromit in a Tiny Home off M22, on West Grand Traverse Bay. It didn't take long for us to fall in love, and every day our bond grows. I take them on long hikes, we snuggle, and they let me sleep in. They don't ask very many questions when we watch movies, and it's always my pick. Being there for my friends has let some of the love I've been asking for in, while spending one of my favorite months alongside big water in one of my favorite places. These headaches are reminding me that I don't have to be the one who holds everything together, and sometimes the only thing left to do is let go.

(the wisdom of frailty)

Grateful for this October downpour and 46-degrees. Aussiedoodles to snuggle, cozy blankets to warm, and windows to gaze through into the wilderness. For the first time in some time, there's no particular place to be. No 4:00 AM alarms, 15-hour-days, or schedules to adhere to. On an exploratory expedition to discover how many days of sleeping in until it becomes the way. Being there for friends by being here; being there for myself by letting go, and doing less. It feels seamless telling others that everything will be okay, yet asks us to dig a little deeper when it's time to tell ourselves. Make time, and take time for that precious beating heart of yours. Let love, warmth, snuggles, hot coffee, and lofi autumn beats into your crevices, bringing you solace by meeting you where you're at for once. You don't have to be that thing you're always compromising. You don't always have to be so alone, to know peace. They say it feels like 33 degrees in Suttons Bay, and I say whatever it feels like is okay with me. My friend Brooke says it's rainbow weather—this Tiny Home is on Rainbows End—what could be better? Sleeping deeper every night, reminding myself that everything will be alright. Thinking of my mom lately, more than most—yesterday was my dad's birthday—I'm grateful we're so close. The love you have carries you when washed over by the love you've lost.

continued

continued

October reminds me that transformation takes time, and trees rarely let go of their leaves all at once. Time is relative and it feels like the rain moves life in slow motion; hypnotizing us like displaced waves of the ocean. A Monet unfolding before our very eyes: water, color, light, and the countryside. Cool, crisp, wet, and alive; an expedition inward to discover our true selves inside. Haven't you ever (always) wondered what wonders you might find?

(An October Monet)

Saturday, October 25. Through the tiny window your watercolor brushstrokes made their way to the bed where I sleep, upstairs in the Tiny Home. You have a way of finding me, when I need you most. Thank you for painting this morning's technicolor sunrise—Appa and I enjoyed it together—snuggled but awake to greet a cool but clear morning on the peninsula. I've made my way to Cedar River Coffee, where I'm greeted with a good sign depicting "joy comes in the morning". We rise and take slow, deep breaths, before exhaling to make space for the budding enthusiasm embedded in the day ahead. Pouring through my second Mary Oliver book, *Upstream,* I know these are the right words, in the right time, in the right place. She talks about the duty and obligation an artist has to its creation, and the frivolity of the ticket collectors mundane routine. Oddly enough, it reminds me of something John Candy once told a young Conan O'Brien when he told him he was thinking about trying comedy when he was his tour guide at Harvard University in 1984: "It's not something you try, you do it, or you don't do it." Mary Oliver knew what John Candy knew, and what Conan O'Brien would eventually learn; we must become what we intend to create. Creativity demands immersion into the wild, spontaneity of life itself—if we have any hope of

continued

continued

depicting such raw wonder in the form of films, poems, paintings, songs, and stories. The raw experience of shifting seas and seasons, from fear to faith, and back again becomes the foundation upon which honest expression captures hearts and imaginations. The real grit of it. People are moved by experiences they believe and can relate to. Some say art comes from love and suffering, but I believe the really good stuff understands that it's the journey between which offers the heartiest sustenance for hungry hearts. Dissonance gives us greater clarity and gratitude for peace. Technicolor sunrises find us where we are looking for their joy and spirit. Displaced loved ones show up for us when we are in a place to receive their presence, wisdom, and love. Art moves us because soul and spirit connect us. Commitment to an uncertain path elevates us because it requires trust. Creation asks for sacrifice because life is precious and fleeting. Each of us is called in a unique direction, and each of us has a choice to be all in or somewhere between. It's alright if you're not called in the ways others are, but each of us has the opportunity to be present, all in, and leading with love. It's not something you try, you do it, or you don't do it.

(watercolor brushstrokes, part 2)

Wavelengths, spectrums, and perspectives. Busyness and volume calls for space and time. Isolation can then comfort, allowing for healing and rest, before calling for connection. Balance, imbalance, ebb and flow. Better knowing one's self supports movement between these wavelengths, with less resistance, and a continually evolving perspective. One could hope that with the passing of each season, comes a deeper and gentler understanding of self, along with a greater appreciation for individual nuance. We are works in progress—certain to regress here or there—along the way. Thus the challenge remains to love ourselves better, anyway. Despite others' effort to impose otherwise upon you, we are not in a hurry, and hurrying rarely makes anything better. Divine timing doesn't ask for patience, but trust. Trust that miracles are unfolding on the timeline they're supposed to. Trust that a greater power is working steadily on your behalf, to give you what you've asked for—even though you cannot see, touch, or taste it yet. Trust that your willingness to embrace uncertainty with an open, full, and kind heart is a key ingredient in the recipe which will transform your dreams into savory, sweet, and succulent food upon your table. Oddly enough, more times than not, grace is the byproduct of a lifetime of collisions. We build, we bend, we bruise, we bleed, we break, we cry, we

continued

continued

learn, and we begin again. Each experience becomes a trail, etched on a map for ourselves and others to guide and return to as needed. Experiences that are most difficult have the tendency to teach us most; and if our burdens become another's blessing, then we're playing our part. Times of learning are often proceeded by flow, abundance, ease, and grace. Balance asks for both stillness and motion. Dreams command discipline. Discipline reveals boundaries. Boundaries reveal space between breaths. Space offers rest. Rest clarifies dreams. Those longings may not be as far away as they seem. Trust that magic is moving on your behalf. Take solace knowing that if it's taking a long time, it's more likely to last. First we learn to trust, then we learn to ask; keep moving forward, let go of the past. Aging is inevitable, ascension is optional, and divinity is eternal: wavelengths, spectrums, and perspectives.

(wavelengths, spectrums, & perspectives)

Somewhere, somebody is having a better day because of my words, my work, and my love—and some days, that's enough. Today feels like one of them. Grateful knowing I'm where I'm supposed to be, while feeling the ease which accompanies alchemy. Alignment feels like home. Flowing comes from sewing our heart's intention, while acknowledging our body's limitations. Rabbit holes are really just research and following through on something you want. What lengths are you willing to go in pursuit of what you love? How much discomfort and uncertainty are you willing to endure whilst your heart's highest hopes make their way to you? This isn't to suggest recklessness, nor dulling your senses to quiet your intuition, rather an arduous yet playful discovery of boundaries. Most of us are really just working on shaping and shifting our edges: learning to be softer on ourselves, less judgmental of others, and move through the changing seasons of our lives with kindness, confidence, and care. This morning I am writing from the kitchen table in this Tiny Home on Rainbows End, looking out across the creek, and through the trees into West Bay. I gave Gromit a light shower after a busy morning parading through the wet wild—he thanks me quietly by sitting at my side—fluffy after a good hair brushing. Just like that it's already been two weeks

continued

continued

of waking up together beside the big water, hiking the many trails, dunes, and beaches of Leelanau, and staying up late to watch all 18 innings of Game 3 of the World Series. This is the most consecutive days I've spent living with dogs on my own, and like many things it came at the perfect time. We continue to sleep in, take naps, exercise, eat treats, and play. My headaches have almost entirely subsided, giving me a greater sense of appreciation and clarity for solitude, balance, and peace. We celebrated a new friend's 31st birthday last night at Three Trees, which continues to feel more and more like a movie, with family reunion vibes. There is a tremendous sense of community here, and I'm thankful to have become a local in my own way. Fall colors have surpassed their peak, the trees are letting go, and giving back to the earth. We make space for what we've asked for, by letting go. We have limited time, bandwidth, and energy to create, connect, communicate, commit, and care. Choose people, activities, communities, and careers that choose and give back to you. Somewhere, somebody is having a better day because of your words, your work, and your love—and some days, I hope that's enough for you to keep doing it.

(somebody, somewhere)

Getting better at choosing me. A few hard moments are a worthy price to pay for falling in love. Some of us spend more time asking for love than others, and it often arrives in different ways than we might expect. I continue to understand gratitude and grace as recognizing the presence of previous prayers, especially when they're subtly nuanced. Sometimes love shows up on a vineyard on a peninsula, in the form of two friends with two aussiedoodles, and a Tiny Home beside a Great Lake. Don't be so far sided, rigid, or foolish that you overlook the blessings before your very eyes, quietly asking for attention. From Oxford to Leelanau, from Leelanau to Japan, and back again: prayers and people pleaded for from the heart—arrive in ways that remind our imaginations to once more stretch and reach for the stars. After all, if the love we ask for has any real hope of a continued stay in our lives, doesn't it make sense that its arrival tells a story that exceeds even our wildest, romantic leanings, inclinations, and imaginations? They tell me that's what true love does, and who am I to doubt the purest substance of my heart, my soul, my story, my stars, and our cosmos? I've learned if we continually yearn to help those we love, we experience living in a way that reminds ourselves and others that we are not alone. We are here for and with one another, simultaneously being and receiving shelter from life's many storms. Some storms we run from, while others we run to—like last night's aurora under the Beaver Moon, aside West Grand Traverse Bay where I've spent almost a month now. My dreams last night reminded me that I am still not where I hope to be, while this morning's breath work in the sauna affirms

continued

continued

little steps and discipline have a magical way of gaining the ground between. I begin today making a water sacrifice and commitment to steadily implement growth, knowing I am ready to slow down, rise, release, and be in one place for a little while. When I make my southern descent it will be with greater peace in my heart, thankful for the opportunity to help carry and receive the love I've been asking for. My body continues to speak to me and I will continue to listen. Often it is the gentle and kind whispers that we refuse to hear, which keeps us from seeing the answers we've been looking for. I hope you're getting better at choosing you. I hope you're discovering that a few hard moments are a worthy price to pay for growing in love. I hope you are reminded that the people who matter want the very best for you. I think we all could benefit from being reminded that better listening is the vehicle most likely to deliver the answers we've been asking for. Grace is a blessing we must first give ourselves.

(sometimes love shows up)

Good morning Oxford—CFE Roasters—how I've missed thee. As it happens, there are lots of places like home, but nothing ever quite feels like returning to yours after an extended time away. We humans love our rituals, our neighborhood coffee shops, and the kind humans who work there. It's a rainy, cool, and damp November morning in Michigan, "Winter Song" by the Head and the Heart plays on the radio, foreshadowing this weekend's incoming snowfall, which will be our first. It is officially cozy season here in the Mitten, and though I've been called Sunshine, I'm here for it. A cup of hot tea under my flannel patterned, fleece blanket, reading Mary Oliver in my heated, massage chair. After close to a month away on Leelanau, I have once more fallen asleep beside, and awoken to be greeted by the view of Oxford Lake. I cherish these November days between Halloween and Thanksgiving, when you hear Christmas carols but change the channel, chuckle at your neighbors who have already put up their lights, thankful for each day the water moves freely before the freeze. We've reached the time of year where it is more common for me to wear socks, though shoes are certainly not certain. Already it feels like my coming months are planned—yet an unexpected text last night from an old friend—reminds me that wonder makes its way into our lives through the most unexpected crevices. November reminds us to hold space and be grateful for the unexpected. It's healthy and necessary to make plans, but that doesn't mean we need to be so rigid that we leave no space for unforeseen, soft, and subtle miracles making their way into our lives. I hope the warmth emitted from the multitude of things that you love, saves you

continued

continued

from growing so cold that you close yourself off from the good news on its way to you. Plot twists are what make good stories great. Rainy days nudge us to seek sunshine in other places. Snowfall welcomes light in a different form. Fallen leaves help us better see the forest for the trees, while revealing a glimpse of what awaits on the other side. Darkness is where stars shine. Loss teaches us to love better. Grief encourages us to be kinder. Sickness insists that we move slower. Music holds our hand no matter what. Blessings come in the form of people. Hunger provides an opportunity to help. Pain asks us to heal. Home makes it easier to. Family understands things take time. The rain knows what it is to lament. The earth empathises with what it is to hurt. The trees can relate to being misunderstood. Nature will persist. Seasons will come and go. Love will endure. Water will find a way. Light will lift. Community will care. Cretins will fall. Crooks will perish. Monday will become Friday and life is seasoned in the days between. How and who will you keep warm with this winter? What is yours that you wish to share with the world? Or maybe just the courage to share it with another? Today I am sharing it with you. Tomorrow I may do the same. Walt Whitman reminds me that the multitudes of who I am will persist, undeterred by a little snow, sleet, or rain.

(rainy day, multitudes)

For all of us humans trying to lose a few pounds, get back in a rhythm, and welcome back the daily blessing of movement: one is something, two is better, and three's a streak. Movement as a daily practice helps us remember to save and apply some of that discipline we so regularly administer, on ourselves. There is great joy in tending to our personal gardens. When we administer care to one place in our daily lives, it has the tendency to spill over into and infuse others where it may have been lacking. Each of us is our own rising tide made better, and lifted higher, with each individual choice to do so. For example, rarely does my writing suffer as a result of choosing to exercise more—whereas the inverse is almost always the case. Letting a little light into even one place where it is lacking, invites great clarity and perspective into the full spectrum of our lives. In some instances we are pretty simple creatures, made better with good habits. Like laughter, good habits are contagious—prompting the release of other practices which may be dimming your light, and holding you back. None of this is to suggest that good habits won't come and go, which they will, just as bad habits do—rather I think I'm just here to remind you that it's okay when they do. If we were lucky we had parents who urged us to get back on our bicycles after we fell down and crashed; exercising is

continued

continued

really no different. Life moves in oscillating waves: back and forth, up and down, highs and lows. Through this process and trajectory we discover that great discipline is required to maintain a particular level of quality and care over a significant period of time. As seasons change, so too do life's circumstances: health, finances, and availability—all of which contribute to the quantity of fucks we're able to give in any particular direction. As they say, "such is life", why not embrace it? Why not be okay with it? Rather than being hard on yourself, why not revel in the abundance with which you're currently moving? Two steps forward, one step back. If you're overwhelmed, it's a good time to make an adjustment. I've found we're the lowest when we want better for ourselves, yet refuse to consistently make choices in the direction of better. Growth is expansion, and expansion teaches us new boundaries (limits). Along with my god given dimensions, I was a very successful athlete as a result of my ability to push limits. Ironically enough, it was my willingness to test those boundaries which ended my career. Grace asks that we grasp, possess, and maintain our healthy limits, or they will be dictated to us by external forces like injury, anxiety, pain, loss, depression, and isolation. On Thursday I ran for the first time

continued

continued

in a while: **something**. Yesterday, I did it again: **better.** After I run today, it will be a **streak**. Whatever it is you've been hoping to invite into your life, today's a good day to do something about it. If it doesn't feel right today, tomorrow's pretty good too. Discover joy tending to your personal garden, and witness it spilling over into the rest of your life. You are a rising tide made better, lifted higher, with each individual choice to do so.

(something, better, streak)

Observe small moments of zen amidst little victories: the warmth of a heated seat as the windshield slowly defrosts; "Good Day Sunshine" playing over the radio to celebrate the anniversary of the 1969 *Life* magazine cover story which dispelled the "Paul Is Dead" hoax; a little boy dressed in blue pajamas named Timmy at the coffee shop who is kindly clearing his mother Abby's mug to the appropriate bin; an otherwise empty room and the availability of your usual corner, window spot. For consecutive days I've greeted first light reading the pages of my brother's new book, "What Turtle Blood Tastes Like", discovering first hand how beautiful it is to read something written by someone you love. Like people, they say books find us at the right time; and like food, I hope everyone discovers what it is to savor pages—intentionally taking your time to prolong an experience you regard as succulent, and sacred. The veil is thinner this time of year and his poetry brings me closer to my family, closer to our past, and closer to myself in acknowledging the distances I've traveled to be who and where I am today. The three most meaningful loves of my life thus far have been baseball, music, and writing—all of which were first his. I guess I really couldn't have asked for a better big brother: He who followed his heart to Alaska, got married

continued

continued

on top of a mountain, introduced me to The Wood Brothers, and Christopher McCandless in my first favorite book. My brother Jonas traveled "Into the Wild" where he started a family, made me an uncle, and began teaching me a lesson each of us will spend our lives learning: what it is to love someone across a great distance. But words on pages transcend space and time, and books are portals to people and places we learn to spend our lives away from. Maybe it is this very distance I've learned to spend my life away from family—which has me better built for grief—and grateful for little victories on cool, November mornings in Michigan. We have only so much space in our lives, why fill it with anything but love? Cast your attention to blessings, and witness them multiply. Celebrate the music, activities, and books you treasure, by acknowledging who helped teach you to cherish them. Grow desire into destiny by expanding your knowledge into the direction you're called to. Learn from older brothers, sisters, uncles, and grandparents. Find your place by bearing witness to the place you currently are, because only you know what it took to get there. Observe small moments of zen amidst little victories: an empty coffee shop now filled with the seasoned artist collective who meets Monday and Friday;

continued

continued

feeling home in an Oxford town that felt so distant and foreign playing baseball here when I was 13; reading poetry on pages that brings me closer to my older brother in Alaska; a plane ticket that helps me spend another Christmas with Papa Lamb; and the accumulated interest of investing my love, into my life. I hope everyone discovers what it is to savor the pages of their lives, intentionally taking time to prolong an experience you regard as succulent, and sacred.

(savoring pages)

I woke this morning comforted by a reminder that we must rise to meet what we've asked for. The greater the ask, the higher we must ascend. Yesterday, on November 11th, around 10:30 pm a magnificent Aurora storm illuminated skies as far south as Alabama. Though the phenomena wasn't visible in Michigan, the Northern Lights danced across the night sky on a calendar day which holds great significance, spiritually. The 11:11 Portal is a global energetic event, where the collective focus on new beginnings and spiritual alignment is at its peak. It is believed to provide access to a powerful gateway for intention, intuition, and manifestation. Are you ready and willing to align with the higher path you're called to? Eventually we learn to ask for what we want in this life, but are we willing to instill the changes necessary to receive the blessings we've called in? Otherwise, their stay will be short-lived, and or overlooked. This is why big dreams take time. Thoreau says the cost of a thing is the amount of life (time, energy, effort) exchanged for it. Discipline requires sacrifice. We must give something up if we intend to invite something in. Our western world seems to be built on competing ethos, where we only let go of something once there is no longer space for it in our lives, homes, or hearts. Perhaps this is why we have such a difficult time letting go of

continued

continued

loved ones. Have we become so poor spiritually that we cling where life is no longer present, in a passive-aggressive effort to defer our grief? The Cree and Inuit believe the Northern Lights are the spirits of loved ones who have passed on, dancing to communicate with the living or to guide them. Others believe they are a celestial bridge between mortals and spirits, connecting us with those who have departed. In Norse mythology, the lights are associated with the Valkyries, female warrior figures who guide fallen heroes to Valhalla. For them, the lights are seen as the reflection from their shields and armor. The Finns believe that the Aurora Borealis symbolize good fortune and prosperity, inviting blessings to those who witness them. Throughout these different cultures is an understanding that the lights serve as a reminder of the delicate balance between the natural world, and the supernatural forces that govern it. Surely ego fuels the fire of man's commitment to separate spirit from science, but even my cousin Gus—the astrophysicist with a PHD on the way—said his studies only offered a limited explanation of what we were experiencing together on the night of the Perseid meteor shower in Suttons Bay. His father, my uncle Arūnas, like my mother, died from pulmonary fibrosis when

continued

continued

Gus was young. It is no coincidence that we experienced one of the most intense Aurora Borealis displays in recent years, together, sitting on the dock of a bay. It was one of the greatest nights of my life, for reasons science cannot explain, and words fail to. But I do acknowledge that I felt my mom's presence more than usual that August night, and choose to believe she and her brother were together again, painting the sky to celebrate that their sons were too.

(aurora borealis)

Another Monday in November, in another year with your spirit displaced. There is a heaviness to these days moving slowly towards Thanksgiving. The weight of the season asks to be embraced with a stillness we've grown unaccustomed to in the busyness of another year. Our sleep grows deeper when we allow ourselves to be embraced by deceleration. You've been visiting me more in dreams as of late, guiding me in your own way. November is reminding me of the catharsis of a good cry; grief is useful in its ability to help us let go of these emotions we carry. It is frightening when the people we love become memories, but over time we discover that timeless emotions are embedded within these memories, and feeling something isn't so different than being together again. Everything we love hurts a little. Stillness allows that hurt to surface, so we may continue to heal. A lot of people try to run from grief, but you're really just running from yourself. We honor the ones we love by finding ways to keep their spirit present in our daily lives. This should look a little different for everyone, and be a reflection of your time together. Moms will do anything to protect you, and tell you how it is. I remember my mom by taking care of myself, loving my family, knowing my worth, and watering my gifts. I see her at sunrise, sunset, and in the Northern Lights. I listen for her in Paul Simon, Roy

continued

continued

Orbison, Rod Stewart, Van Morrison, and Otis Redding. There is no replacing the spaces she occupies within my heart, so I do my best to acknowledge them, and carry her spirit with me. As the weight of this holiday season settles upon you—I hope you discover the magic of looking to—and not away from the memories you made together. Listen to their favorite songs, watch their favorite movies, and carry on their favorite traditions. A soul's greatest triumph is the positive imprint it leaves on the lives it blesses in whatever amount of time they get to share together. Too many memories of my mom have grown quiet in the distance, but maybe I'm just learning to better listen for her voice when it accompanies blessings on the horizon. Some celebrations happen in empty rooms, just as some joy comes from the last places we look. We carry some memories forever—without ever really being certain why—while others we hope to hold onto, slowly slip away. Maybe those we've let go are just making space for something new. Afterall, new experiences have a funny way of stirring memories we believed to be lost. Maybe holding on, means letting go. Maybe letting go is a great indicator that we've grown. Maybe it happened even if we didn't know it could. Maybe along the way we learned to help others do the same. It

continued

continued

is frightening when the people we love become memories, but that doesn't mean they're gone. Everything we love hurts a little, but that doesn't mean we love any less. Forgotten isn't lost. We can feel someone's presence, even if we can't hold them in our arms. When life gets really heavy, remember to move more slowly. When it feels like you can no longer hold on, maybe it's time to let go.

(when people become memories)

Jake and Morgan remind us that love is real and it's up to you how you choose to celebrate it. Marriage should be about you—while reflecting the time you've spent together thus far—and the life you're setting the intention to live. If you're called to an island in the Caribbean, the ones who hope to keep you in their lives will find a way to be there. Presence is achieved in a multitude of different ways. Love can show up for love without getting on a plane. Love can provide the perfect gift without breaking the bank. Love asks each of us to show up in our own way. Some are better at it than others, but it doesn't mean it's easy. Performance is a reflection of practice. Kindness is a demonstration of empathy. Find your own way to show up and be there for the ones you love. It is worth the cost, and designed to help you feel better. Morgan and Jake's friendship has always helped me feel better. They understand the quiet I need in storms I had grown too accustomed to sailing in. They took time to come to my home and meet me where I'm at. I suspect they've done something similar for you in their own way. Spend time with and celebrate people who help you be and feel better. Find a way to be on an island in the Caribbean with them when they get married on a mountain. Find ways to be there for yourself more frequently, so you too can witness love and beautiful

continued

continued

collisions that take flight. You don't need a flight plan, but practice and experience help. You don't need to be rich, but it helps when your presence demonstrates the generosity of your spirit. In most instances in life, multiple truths accompany one another. It can be about you and them. It's most consistently best for myself and others. When one person finds love in the world, two people's love raises humanity's understanding of love exponentially. Let yourself take small, quiet steps, and receive exponential blessings.

(jake and morgan)

Since most of us are lonely in one way or another—it feels like a good time to learn how to better speak to one another—and the best place to begin is learning to better listen. Listening doesn't mean taking a punch for a punch. Listening doesn't mean not so patiently refraining from speaking while allowing someone else to speak. Listening is the most elegant yet simple form of love. Listening means giving a shit, consistently, and especially when the delivered contents have nothing to do with you. Listening is philosophy. Listening is a martial art. Listening is therapy. Listening is a remedial test parents give their children before trusting them to swim without drowning. Loneliness stems from disconnection. Our failure to connect breeds loneliness. Belonging is born from connection. Connection inspires community. Community offers belonging by way of its ability to listen and hear. Listening eases the tension of loneliness. Loneliness amplifies our desire for good conversation. Good conversation is built on listening and reciprocity. Reciprocity is another word for balance. Some of us learn the miracle of moderation on our journey to discover balance. Balance helps us understand both sides of the beam. Practice is the foundation of philosophy. A personal philosophy helps change how we see and why we see it. Perspective teaches us that

continued

continued

loneliness is a symptom of freedom. Freedom teaches us that balance comes from discipline. Discipline reveals what we're capable of. Capability invites us to aim higher. Empathy teaches us how to help others do the same. Listening reveals how we can show up for others. Showing up for others increases the likelihood of having people who will listen in your time of need. When you grow weary from loneliness, reach out to the people you've shown up for. If you find yourself with no one who will listen, maybe it's time to start showing up.

(listening)

Just because someone's good at it, doesn't mean it's easy. Just because someone cares, doesn't mean they have to. Most people are who they are as a result of a lifetime of choices. Observe, appreciate, and honor those choices. Let other people's steady choices help you make your own. Let good people make impressions on you, but don't be too hard on yourself because we all arrive when we're supposed to. Arrive in your own way. Appreciate your own time. Shed some grace your own way along the journey. Ask yourself what you want. Don't so readily accept and absorb what others tell you that you should want. Be playful and have fun. Remember there is a time and place for all things. Try to be present no matter where you are. Be thankful for those who help you feel home. Learn to help others feel the same. Grow your tribe once you find it. Remember it is easier to find when we seek it, even though sometimes the best things in life find us when we stop looking for them. Life is a paradox. God works in contradictions. Tomorrow is likely, though not promised. Your choices add or subtract meaning from your life. Make math your friend. Simplify with care. Build with intent. Grow with grace. Spend more time doing what you're good at, but don't be afraid to try something new. Root to rise. Feel to flourish. Face and embrace the music. Go your own way. Carry with

continued

continued

kindness. Falter with a sense of humor. Be honest with yourself. Make better choices more often. Acknowledge how far you've come. Be thankful the journey continues. Revel in the sunshine today. Remember it will return when it fades. Just because someone's good at it, doesn't mean it's easy; and just because something is taking its time, doesn't mean it's not on its way.

(on our way)

It feels like a lot of people are being asked to fly with broken wings these days. It's not impossible, it's just difficult—while sucking an extra fat one because in many cases comes as a result of institutional failure. Our elected government is at war with its people, bringing tyranny to the streets at the hands of fascists, under the guise of national security, and public safety. I don't know about you, but shooting and in some instances killing unarmed civilians in the street doesn't make me feel safer. Call me a bleeding Liberal if it helps you feel better, but I think for myself and my diet doesn't include being shovel-fed horse shit from Fox News. The machine swiftly moves to discredit and dehumanize Renee Nicole Good, a 37-year-old mother of three, prize-winning poet, and hobby guitarist. Good was not an activist nor domestic terrorist. She was a devoted Christian who traveled to Ireland on youth missions when she was younger. Previously, she worked as a dental assistant and at a credit union before becoming mostly a stay-at-home mom in recent years. Almost a year ago she came to Minneapolis with her wife and six-year-old child to find a place where they could find community and be comfortable. Good studied creative writing at Old Dominion University in Norfolk, Virginia, and in 2020 she won an undergraduate prize from the Academy of American Poets for her piece entitled *On Learning to Dissect Fetal Pigs*. We are witnessing weaponized hate, violence, and fascism for profit. Every day Americans struggle with the reality that its government demonstrates more concern with immigration enforcement, than it does supporting the well-being of the people it exists to serve. I was listening to the

continued

continued

radio on my way to the coffee shop this morning when a man requested "Black Bird" from The Beatles, because it was his deceased father's favorite song, and whenever he and his son heard it, they felt closest to him. From their 1968 double album *The Beatles*—also known as "the White Album"—it was written by Paul McCartney after hearing the call of a blackbird in Rishikesh, India, and by the civil rights movement in the Southern United States. Widely regarded as one of the best songs by The Beatles, McCartney wanted to write a song dedicated to people who had been affected by discrimination: "The unjust or prejudicial treatment of different categories of people, especially on the grounds of ethnicity, age, sex, or disability." Almost sixty years later fear and fascism continue to divide us into different categories of people, either unwilling or afraid to think for ourselves, serve God, honor life, demand more, and speak to the true evil running wild in the streets, infecting us with disease. George Orwell says "In a time of deceit, telling the truth is a revolutionary act." The heart of corruption is a misallocation of resources. The American people would benefit from a reallocation of resources. Lives could be made better, and in many instances saved with a rational, spiritual, and essential shift in how our leaders understand what security and public safety actually means to its people who rely on those resources, versus serving the agenda of a select few. What are we so afraid of? Where is the love? Where is the decency? Where has humanity strayed while we fight these same old,

continued

continued

tired, despicable, and cowardice battles in our streets? We are here to help carry one another; to be at service of one another; and to help pick up the pieces and build something better together. I know it feels like a lot of people are being asked to fly with broken wings right now, and maybe that's how we fight for Good.

(fight for Good)

But how do we fly with broken wings you may wonder? It starts with keeping our hearts open, our feet moving, and the choice to keep on going. In the song "Thin Blue Flame" by Josh Ritter he says, "You need faith for the same reason it's so hard to find." Malice does not deserve malice, but it does necessitate accountability. We must allow space, time, and pause for the way malice, ill will, and corruption makes us feel, so we may be accountable to ourselves and others to identify acts and actors whose actions are void of love. We find a way to see things for the way they are, not how they or we hope them to be. We listen to what others need, and how we can help them. We stop pretending like we have all of the answers, when clearly this isn't working. You're ignorant to your addiction if you cannot acknowledge that we have a problem. If you're hurting more than usual right now, that's good, it means you're human. If you're like me you're finding your way to peace in your heart—so we may honor those who have come before—by better helping and serving one another going forward. Each of us finds, connects, and nourishes community in our own way. We are drawn to places and people where and who remind us that the prevailing spirit of humanity is good. We share pieces of ourselves as daily bread on the table to help fill and sustain people hungry for a better way. Not because we are obligated, but because we are able. It is this ability that connects us to the people and lives we came here to experience. Pride is a derivation of purpose and belonging. Your abilities are your North Star navigating you in the direction of your people and place. German composer and pianist Robert Schuman says "To send light into the

continued

continued

darkness of men's hearts—such is the duty of the artist." May we fight the urge to let our hearts grow cold and condemn, allowing ourselves a chance to heal, so we too may illuminate the darkness of men's hearts. Save and savor your strength. May we allow ourselves the bread and breath we need, before answering malice with a broken mirror. Broken things become beautiful things when we help them. Each of us has a stake and place in this, and there's work to be done. More than ever it's imperative to be mindful of who and where you are giving your energy and attention. Give yourself this time to revel in who and what you love. Trust that no one is more worthy of it than yourself. Consider all those you have helped feed with your daily bread. Take faith knowing how many others are on their way with an offering to the table. Try to be patient knowing how many are doing their best to fly with broken wings. Be humble when you learn to. This is how we fly with broken wings. It starts with keeping our hearts open, our feet moving, and the choice to keep on hoping.

(broken wings)

Last night I tried something new, and today I'm better for it. For the first time in roughly 15 years I attended a yoga class. More specifically, Candlelight Yin Yoga at The Giving Tree Collective. The first, and only other yoga class I attended was Bikram or Vinyasa Yoga (hot yoga)—which was not for me. My friend Micha who was on the dance team at Michigan State took me. I remember sweating profusely, being restricted by my boardshorts (wrong clothing choice), while being extraordinarily uncomfortable in a room with humans far more advanced than I. As a former competitive athlete (baseball, basketball) with the likeness of a viking, flexibility and stretching have always been those things I need yet deny myself of. Like anything, consistency is key. At 6'7 and 285 pounds, gravity continues to teach me of the toll it takes to move mountains. Most commonly in the form of a pinched sciatic nerve. I learned about yin yoga from a friend, who helped me trust that it was a more approachable, and accessible practice. Stemming from Taoism and Traditional Chinese Medicine, yin yoga's philosophy focuses on balancing yin (passive, cool, feminine) and yang (active, warm, masculine) energies through long-held, floor-based poses that target deep connective tissues. It's a meditative practice emphasizing stillness, surrender, and awareness while

continued

continued

working on the body's deeper yin structures to enhance flexibility and promote energetic balance. Unlike dynamic yoga (yang), yin yoga's long holds (3-5+ minutes) apply gentle, sustained stress to fascia, ligaments, and joints, making them longer, stronger, and more supple. I came in with the intention to be okay with wherever I was at in my flexibility and comfort with the poses. I empathize with the difficulty of letting go and focusing on breath while expanding boundaries and trying something new. Of the eight or so poses we held in the one hour class, I was comfortable with and had practiced about half on my own. The other half were not outrageous or unreasonable, my body simply showed me that those are areas that would benefit from more practice. Thankfully, those poses can be aided by tools like pillows and blankets which are not only available on hand, but encouraged. Having to do fewer overall poses, held in place longer, made it much easier for me to quiet my mind, listen to our instructor's voice, appreciate the music, and feel at home with myself in my practice. Even though it was a well attended class, in a mostly filled room, an emphasis to practice with our eyes closed helped me be less self-conscious and more self-aware. Every now and again I would open my eyes to confirm or deny that I was holding the

continued

continued

instructed pose, which I found useful, but also comforting that it didn't really matter. What mattered is that I was in the room, trying something new that I've always known is good for me. Not only making time for my own peace and balance, but pushing the boundaries of my comfort level to experience new depths within myself. For the first time in my life I own a yoga mat and intend to attend a weekly yin yoga class. I will continue doing cardio and stretching at the gym, enjoying this as another layer in my physical, mental, and spiritual wellness. If you're yoga curious, experience sciatica, or maybe are just looking for an intentional place to access community and breathe, yin yoga is a pretty good place to begin. It's never too late to try something new, and it's difficult to go somewhere you've never been unless you do.

(yin yoga)

MY SUNSHINE

If joy is a protest
love is a sacrifice
commitment through practice
consistency amidst chaos
sunshine on a cold winter day
words with something to say
hands with someone to hold
blessings to be shared
a quiet reminder someone cares
because caring can be enough
on those days we need a little love
kindness is its own super power
readily available and sometimes hard to find
hardened hearts easily divide
helping hands change lives
corruption needs minions to sell lies
bigots to deputize
spirit speaks through open eyes
joy doesn't need to wear a disguise
love doesn't victimize
love is a sacrifice
shared in service
learned in practice
gardening goodness
bearing witness
condemning the heartless
honoring creation's kiss
opposing godlessness
standing up for kids
being human and giving a shit

(being human and giving a shit)

Many of us are feeling the great weight of injustice, ignorance, and absurd cruelty which we had previously only read about in books. It has a way of making you feel helpless, even though we're not. It has a way of asking you to appreciate and be grateful for the privilege, blessings, and opportunities you have, as we observe them being stripped from and denied to others. What's happening in this nation before our very eyes, has been happening behind closed doors for a very long time. I read a poem about two moms packing their kid's lunch for school. The first mom packed a juice, a banana, and a note that says "I love you". The second mom packed "A copy of her child's birth certificate, a number to call if the silence becomes too long, and the unspoken knowledge of what it might mean to disappear." Imagine what it is like to be that child, or that child's mother right now. Imagine if this nation was led with that type of courage, instead of such extraordinary cowardice and delusion. For the first time in my life the qualities that exemplify humanity as either beautiful or dangerous, have never been so obvious, and neglected. We are simultaneously being asked to observe the miracle of life, in juxtaposition to its frailty when possessed by evil men with wickedness in their hearts. It's a little like winter in that regard: it's beautiful—but if you're not

continued

continued

prepared—it might kill you. Martin Luther King, Jr. fought the same battle in the Deep South that is being fought in Minneapolis today. Federal agents are acting outside of their legal rights to provide enforcement that Governor Tim Walz has refused. History repeats itself, and yet again a cruel, heavy handed dictator serves his best interest while denying the rights and due process of the very laws and democracy which elected him. We tell ourselves that something has to give, and we hope it does, but many of us have difficulty understanding how we arrived here in the first place. These are not easy times, but great conflict has a way of bringing divided people closer together. That is the greatest benefit of a true villain. When great struggle is met with a collective, communal response, people are empowered by their choice to rise. Initially it may feel like we are rising on the behalf of others, but ultimately we discover that within our ascension, resides our destiny. We begin to understand that if it's happening to one of us, it could be happening to any of us. So please, continue to take care of yourself and listen in the direction you're called. Be grateful for the warmth you know and can depend on this winter, but keep your eyes and heart open. Humanity has been here before and we will likely be here

continued

continued

again, yet still, your response to the great weight of injustice, ignorance, and absurd cruelty can be entirely unique. You have the ability to think and feel for yourself. You have the opportunity to help in the ways you know how. You can honor the courage of mothers and children who go to school each day, not knowing if the notes carried in lunch boxes will be the last time they ever speak.

(what it might mean to disappear)

For the second time in 17 days, ICE Agents unlawfully killed a law-abiding US citizen in the streets of Minneapolis. Thirty-seven-year-old Alex Jeffrey Pretti, RN, was an ICU nurse with the Veterans Administration (VA), gunned down by ICE while engaging in his lawful right to observe and document the ongoing violation of human rights in Minneapolis. Dr. Aasma Shaukat, who hired Pretti at Minneapolis VA Health Care System about a decade ago, told the Washington Post that he was one of the sweetest, kindest, gentlest souls that she'd ever met. Shaukat added that Pretti "always stood for people and human rights, helping fellow citizens and just being a good citizen of society and the communities that he lived in". Of the videos circulating on the incident, Shaukat told The Post "It just feels so wrong. Knowing Alex, he was probably trying to protect or help or shield somebody from the agents. He had not a single mean bone in his body; always spoke about doing the right thing." The Minnesota Organization of Registered Nurses (MNORN) released a statement about Pretti's death that said: "Today, our nursing community is grieving. We have lost a fellow registered nurse to an act of violence connected to immigration enforcement. Regardless of where each of us stands on the issues surrounding this moment, the loss of a

continued

continued

nurse, a caregiver, a colleague, a human being cuts us deeply. This message is not about politics. It is about mourning a life taken too soon and honoring the calling we all share. As nurses, we understand loss in a way others may not understand. We know how quickly life can change, how fragile safety can feel, and how pain reaches far beyond one individual to families, coworkers, patients, and communities. When one nurse is lost, all of us feel it." Dedicated to serving veterans, it is a nurse's job to care for their patients but they are also ethically bound to speak out in the face of injustice and human rights violations. Provision 8.2 of the American Nurses Association Code of Ethics for Nurses states, "Where there are human rights violations, nurses ought to and must stand up for those rights and demand accountability." Accustomed to affording others grace and dignity in their most vulnerable moments, it is consistent with Pretti's character that in his final act he came to the aid and defense of a female citizen being brutalized by ICE. Videos from the incident reveal that ICE removed Pretti's firearm from its holster, prior to firing 10 gun shots and rendering him lifeless in the street. Minneapolis Police Chief Brian O'Hara said that Pretti was a legal gun owner and did not have a criminal record. His

continued

continued

next-door neighbor, Jeanne Wiener, told The New York Times "He's the sweetest, kindest, most unoffensive, most nonviolent person you'd ever want to meet." Ruth Anway, who worked with Mr. Pretti described him as a passionate colleague and kindhearted friend with a sharp sense of humor. "He cared about people deeply and he was very upset with what was happening in Minneapolis and throughout the United States with ICE, as millions of other people are upset," said Michael Pretti, Alex's father. "He thought it was terrible, you know, kidnapping children, just grabbing people off the street. He cared about those people, and he knew it was wrong, so he did participate in protests" (Associated Press). Are these the type of people our government claims to be keeping us safe from? Are the kindness, service, and courage of Alex Jeffrey Pretti the ideals that Donald Trump wages war against? How many American citizens will be kidnapped, tear gassed, and killed in the streets before we regard preserving life as a greater priority than anyone's misguided politics? Has your comfortable bubble been challenged yet? When you read about Nicole Good and Alex Pretti being killed in the street by ICE, have you felt that feeling in your gut knowing it could have been your daughter, son, sister, brother, mother, father, or friend? In

continued

continued

the quiet when no one's watching, have you listened to your heart and questioned what they might say about you or the ones you love, while painting their picture of domestic terrorism? Why is it that it takes a nurse to be killed before nurses stand up to such flagrant violations of human rights? This isn't a slant against nurses, rather a plea to what makes us each human; a plea to remember that before we are Americans, Democrats, Republicans, nurses, teachers, writers, or politicians, we are human beings. The wrongful, unnecessary, and avoidable claim upon any life, is a stake in the heart of the sanctity and blessing of all living things. What was once an American Dream, has become an American Illusion. If you don't think this is your battle, then consider it's your ignorance they depended on, and ignorance itself which makes our present reality possible. It's never too late to change your mind, or maybe just listen to your heart. Peaceful, diverse, and thriving communities have been transformed into war zones under the guise of homeland security. Despite fear's best effort to govern the streets of Minneapolis, hundreds of thousands of Minnesotans continue to peacefully gather, protest, and love thy neighbor while standing against and observing an administration that has chosen reckless policy,

continued

continued

inflammatory rhetoric, and manufactured crisis over responsible leadership and de-escalation. Who is being served and protected with this misappropriation of power and resources? When did obscuring and discrediting truth become mission critical in this nation's commitment to and collaboration with fascist propaganda? How have faith-claiming people willingly accepted such distinct boundaries and limits for just who is deserving of God's love? When did your perspective of freedom become so obtuse, limited only to those who agree with you or the current regime? Whether you've acknowledged it or not yet, we are witnessing a pivotal point in the history of the world. Years from now when you look back over your life, when you speak to your children, and grandchildren, I hope you're able to honestly say that you cared deeply for others, stood for human rights, and defended the vulnerable in their time of need like Alex Pretti did. Opposition knows many roads. Peace is practiced over many paths. Silence is a form of compliance. Violence is rhetoric for tyrants. This isn't the way.

(Alex Jeffrey Pretti)

It's easy to be worn down by the bleakness of winter. It's easy to be afraid of hardened hearts, and the ongoing reality of ICE brutality in the streets. It's easy to retreat from a world that seems so intent on burning. It's easy to look away. It's easy to be consumed by our own problems. It's easy to forget how much harder others have it. It's easy to mistake an ancient injustice as something new. It's easy to forget the people, nations, and tribes swallowed by colonization. It's easy to regard the United States as morally superior to genocide—even if it means denying the past—and refusing to acknowledge the present. It's easy to feel like your voice doesn't matter, in a world run by morally reprehensible people and crooks. It's easy to forget what it feels like to be marginalized or bullied. It's easy to pull punches and play it safe when truth is being persecuted. Some things in life are easier than others. For example, it's difficult to hear good, loving humans like Nicole Good and Alex Pretti be called domestic terrorists. It's difficult to have faith in a Republican Party intent on persecuting people because of the color of their skin. It's difficult to understand how poorly trained, disgraceful ICE agents receive $40k checks as signing bonuses without having any accountability to balance their rule. It's difficult to accept that decent, educated, and religious

continued

continued

Americans are unable or unwilling to acknowledge that our government is lying to us, breaking the law, and purposely occupying domestic soil to instigate fear and serve its own agenda of profit motive. It's difficult to believe that enough Americans think what's going on in this country is great. It's difficult to accept that this is what you thought (hoped) you were voting for. It's difficult to empathize with how much you must be hurting, to think others deserve to endure such pain and cruelty. It's difficult to consider the eternal winter you must be carrying in your heart, to have grown so cold and numb to basic human conditions. It's difficult to look a nation in the eyes who denies the ethos it was founded upon. It's difficult to have hope in a nation whose school system is best characterized by gun violence. It's difficult to tell children that everything is going to be okay, when everything else suggests otherwise. It's difficult to have faith, when so many refuse reason and accountability. It's easy to let hate harden your heart. It's easy to grow cold from the ways of the wicked. It's easy to resist emotions that make you uncomfortable. It's easy to be a sheep, and go with the flow. It's easy to point fingers instead of offering a helping hand. It's easy to wear a mask, and be a thug with tear gas and a gun on the street. It's easy to

continued

continued

let other people think and speak for you. It's easy to go to church on Sunday, but participation is not testimony of the strength of your spirit, nor willingness to help others in their time of need. It's easy to look away, but courage asks you to look within. It's easy to think you can't make a difference, but you can. It's easy to walk away—yet every day—people are showing up. It's never too late to start showing up. There are so many ways to show up. It's never too late to look to, and lead with love. It's never too late to try letting a little light in, it has a way of warming you in places grown numb. It's difficult to acknowledge human rights for some, but not everyone. It's difficult to explain equality, based on how this nation is being run. It's difficult to witness fascism in the land of the free, experiencing the miracle of life and death, under the same sun.

(it's easy to look away)

Standing up for what you believe in isn't political, it's decent. Standing up for others isn't activism, it's community. Protesting isn't terrorism, it's patriotism. Before all else the government exists to serve and protect its people. Authoritarianism is a form of government characterized by highly concentrated power, suppressed dissent, and the rejection of democratic checks and balances. It prioritizes top-down control, often enforcing submission through intimidation, restricted civil liberties, and manipulation of information. Those resisting the obvious truth right now—like things the way they are—most likely because they don't know any better. It's an important time for each of us to consider the ways we could be better. Fear intends to isolate, stifle, and deflate the spirit of a people. We are the people. We are demonstrating that we can be afraid while still showing up for one another, and holding love in our hearts. We are learning the depths of our collective naivety, while witnessing the rise of protagonists in the form of everyday people who are giving their lives in the service of others. We are hearing children, students, young men, and young women stand up and testify in solidarity on behalf of immigrant classmates and friends. They speak to the crushing weight of living and learning in an environment where they are always afraid. They are asking for

continued

continued

accountability from a president who offers none. They are standing up against, and walking out on ICE brutality. Is it so unreasonable that they ask for an inkling of the same from this nation's leadership? Is it unreasonable to ask an agent of the law to perform their duties without murdering people in the streets? Is it unreasonable to ask a nation founded on immigration, to honor the due process of the immigration laws it set in place? Is it unreasonable to offer a helping hand to a woman being pushed and tear gassed in the streets? Is it unreasonable to acknowledge that methods deployed in Minneapolis and other cities around the United States are not adherent to the Constitution, nor in the best interest of the communities they're occupying? I'm not asking you to stand between an armed ICE agent and a vulnerable human being in the street, but for the love of the god you claim, do consider being reasonable, helpful, and kind. The soul of humanity is enduring spiritual warfare, making it an essential time for each of us to align with our ethics, empathy, and higher power. It's pretty easy to identify when a government becomes more concerned with censoring, than serving its people. Journalists are detained. Videos clearly revealing one thing, are said to be another. Good humans, and citizens are slandered as domestic

continued

continued

terrorists. A spiritual war is a war on truth. It's the house betting on us being divided, so we inevitably fall. We are not at war with anyone other than ourselves. We don't have to bring each other down. We don't have to meet their low expectations of us. We don't have to drink the poison, and we certainly don't need to offer it to others on their behalf. Standing up for what you believe in isn't political, it's decent. Standing up for others isn't activism, it's community. Protesting isn't terroism, it's patriotism. Before all else the government exists to serve and protect its people. Independent of your ties and allegiances, do you feel that your best interests are being served and protected right now? If not, what are you willing to do about it? Starting anywhere, is somewhere, and now would be a good time.

(before all else)

It's a good time to think for yourself. It's a good time to create something new. It's a good time to be kind. It's a good time to observe who others are showing themselves to be. It's a good time to acknowledge that we do not have all of the answers. It's a good time to distance yourself from hate. It's a good time to renounce racism. It's a good time to learn something new. It's a good time to acknowledge there are better ways to do things. It's a good time to be empathetic of women and people of color. It's a good time to listen to women and people of color. It's a good time to read a history book. It's a good time to read a book written by someone whose background is different from your own. It's a good time to notice how people and places make you feel. It's a good time to distance yourself from people who lack reason and empathy. It's a good time to consider what community means to you. It's a good time to celebrate diversity. It's a good time to be hardworking in the name of something or someone you love and believe in. It's a good time to expand our boundaries. It's a good time to wonder why things are the way they are. It's a good time to believe that they don't always have to be. It's a good time to be there for a friend. It's a good time to help a stranger. It's a good time to speak up for someone being spoken down to. It's a good time to be thankful for all of the good people in our

continued

continued

lives. It's a good time to let go of those who continue to demonstrate otherwise. It's a good time to practice what we preach, and be impatient with cruelty. It's a good time to honor your feelings. It's a good time to listen to your gut. It's a good time to support a local band. It's a good time to eat at an ethnic restaurant. It's a good time to consider how our government spends our money. It's a good time to wonder why our government seems to make so few things better. It's a good time to let them know how you feel about their performance. It's a good time to discover your voice. It's a good time to honor that everyone has one. It's a good time to use discernment with regard to who we listen to. It's a good time to consider what—who we listen to—says about us. It's a good time to use our voices in opposition to tyranny. It's a good time to discredit imbeciles. It's a good time to accept that sometimes broken things need to get worse, before they get better. It's a good time to trust that feeling which insists you deserve better. It's a good time to try things that help you feel better. It's a good time to support people who help you be better. It's a good time for everyday people like you and I—to work for something better.

(good time)

With special thanks to my friend Clay Dodson.

Kevin Alan Lamb is a hopeful romantic, author, and poet based in Oxford, Michigan. Known to many as 6'7 Kevin, a friendly giant with a big heart, he writes inspirational poetry and prose that move like music—rooted in love, healing, and alignment. He is the author of *Ele Phan-Te*, *Love Vigilante*, *Love Is in the Details*, *Your Daily Guide to Shine*, and *The Dying Romantic*, inviting readers to embrace life's flow, soften into self-love, and rise in their own quiet power.

We are a rising tide comprised of old souls, shooting stars, and hungry hearts. An underdog story fueled by empathy, forged in fire, and written in love. We have been battered and we have been broken, only to discover the strength awoken from such depths. The world has shattered our armor, helping us discover that cracks are where the light comes in. Our ships have been swallowed by raging seas in the dead of night, teaching us how to tread water just long enough to be saved by rescue boats in the coming dawn. They told us to have dreams so we held them in our hearts long enough to learn how beautiful and terrifying that it can be, to carry something you love that much. We are a testament of endurance, a deep ocean current, carrying the best of yesterday into the imagination of tomorrow. A reminder that you will never have to do it alone, because each of us understands what it feels like to carry a weight too great to bear.

www.ingramcontent.com/pod-product-compliance
Lightning Source LLC
Chambersburg PA
CBHW032231080426
42735CB00008B/797